Designing & Living with *Glass Tiles*

Inspiration for Home and Garden

Patricia Hart McMillan, Liz Hart McMillan, Katharine Kaye McMillan, PhD

Schiffer Publishing Ltd®

4880 Lower Valley Road Atglen, Pennsylvania 19310

Published by Schiffer Publishing Ltd.
4880 Lower Valley Road
Atglen, PA 19310
Phone: (610) 593-1777; Fax: (610) 593-2002
E-mail: Info@schifferbooks.com

For the largest selection of fine reference books on this and related subjects, please visit our web site at
www.schifferbooks.com
We are always looking for people to write books on new and related subjects. If you have an idea for a book please contact us at the above address.

This book may be purchased from the publisher.
Include $5.00 for shipping.
Please try your bookstore first.
You may write for a free catalog.

In Europe, Schiffer books are distributed by
Bushwood Books
6 Marksbury Ave.
Kew Gardens
Surrey TW9 4JF England
Phone: 44 (0) 20 8392 8585; Fax: 44 (0) 20 8392 9876
E-mail: info@bushwoodbooks.co.uk
Website: www.bushwoodbooks.co.uk

Cover photo by Federico Cedrone, courtesy Bisazza, page 88
Back cover photo courtesy Sicis, pages 124-125

Other Schiffer Books by Patricia Hart McMillan, Liz Hart McMillan, Katharine Kaye McMillan, PhD
Glass Tile Inspirations for Kitchens and Baths. ISBN: 0764325094. $19.95.

Other Schiffer Books on Related Subjects
Beautiful Bathrooms. Tina Skinner. ISBN: 0764315366. $24.95
Best of Today's Interior Design. Tina Skinner. ISBN: 9780764331893. $49.99
Designer Showcase: Interior Design at its Best. Melissa Cardona and Nathaniel Wolfgang-Price. ISBN: 0764323989. $44.95
Inspired High-End Interior Design. Shane Reilly. ISBN: 0764324993. $44.95
Tile Style for the Home: Kitchens, Baths, and More. Tina Skinner, with the Spanish Ceramic Tile Manufacturer's Association. ISBN: 9780764327735. $24.95

Library of Congress Control Number: 2009923679

Covers and Book Designed by: Bruce Waters
Type set in Snell Roundhand Bld/Humanist 521 BT

ISBN: 978-0-7643-3266-1
Printed in China

Contents

Acknowledgments....4

Introducing Glass Tile....5

One: Glass Tile Style for Home & Garden....7

- All Through The House....7
  - Traditional....7
  - Contemporary....10
- In The Garden....15

Two: Color....24

- Metallics....29
- Red....37
- Pink....45
- Green....51
- Blue....60
- Good-Earth Tones....74
- Neutrals....83

Three: Pattern....96

Four: Face Value—Finish and Texture....130

Five: Sizes and Shapes....152

Six: Installing Glass Tile Tips....172

Seven: Sources....176

Acknowledgments

To all who so cheerfully joined forces with us to create this book, we offer heartfelt thanks and deep admiration for your part in creating the wonderful world of glass tile.

Riccardo Bisazza
Carolyn Brown
Cyndi Burkey
Ken Burkey
Alexandra Bursac
Izabel Burbridge
Rerisson Carvalho
Barbara Cashman
Spencer Davidson
Dacia Delgado
Allison Goldenstein
Jordan Goldstein
Karen Gustafson
Mariel Hartoux
Mike Hauner
Angela Hood
Linda Jennings
Grace Kalina
David Knox
Julian Laverde
Helen Lesley
Ola Lessard
Rita Levine
Susan Grant Lewin
JoAnn Locktov
Jan MacLatchie
Ann Britt Malden
Joseph McKenna
Christine O'Dea
Lesley Provenzano
Denise Quasius
Julie Richey
Priscilla Santos
Rudy Santos
Craig Spenser
Elisa Stocchetti
Karen Story
Betty Sullivan
Alicia Tapp
Debbie Thompson

Introducing Glass Tile

Beauty and brawn make glass tile an ideal surface for home and garden

The *magic* of glass is its extraordinary beauty.

Photographs, no matter how marvelous, are no substitute for the heady experience of handling glass tile. The superb photography in this book will surely inspire visits to showrooms to see and examine this amazing, uniquely *interactive* surfacing material. For while other materials *reflect* light, glass tile *refracts* light, creating compelling movement, and engaging the viewer as a partner in its exhilarating dance with light. To make locating and visiting glass tile showrooms easier, Chapter Seven, Sources, lists the manufacturers who have supplied images and information for *Designing and Living With Glass Tile*.

The *miracle* of glass is its practicality

Glass only looks fragile. Thanks to new technology, much glass is suitable for outdoor use as patio flooring, walkways, and exterior walls—even in cold climates. It adds sparkle to pools, fountains, garden walls, and outdoor furniture.

Indoors, beauty and practicality join forces to make glass the new *must-have* surface for walls and floors in high-traffic, frequent-use areas such as entry halls, passageways, bathrooms, and kitchens.

Interestingly, beautiful natural stone is thought to be indestructible, ideal for flooring and countertops. But natural stone is porous and must be sealed in order to resist moisture and stain. Glass tile is vitreous, non-porous, does not absorb moisture or stains, and needs no sealant.

Some fear that glass tile is breakable. It is. But no material likes hard knocks. Ceramic tile cracks and chips. And when clay-based tile is chipped, the exposed porous clay underbody absorbs moisture and stains. Even natural stone can chip, and over time it wears down.

The protective colorful glaze covering ceramic tiles can wear away. But color is integral to cast and fused glass. It cannot wear off. Color in these tiles stands up to UV rays and does not fade—a godsend for glass-walled rooms.

Newly popular for residential use, glass mosaics are an ancient material with a rich history. The much-visited San Marco Cathedral in Venice (Figure 38), with its gleaming gold mosaics is, literally, a shining example. The beauty of the San Marco mosaics is maintained by the Orsoni company, founded in 1888 by Angelo Orsoni (Figure 1). The founder's great, great-grandson, master mosaic artist Lucio Orsoni, has continued the great traditions of the company and of glass tile mosaic artistry. Mosaic artists worldwide flock to his Master Class in the mosaic arts.

Figure 1. The Color Library of the legendary Angelo Orsoni Company in Venice, Italy, houses archives of thousands of colors of glass for the master glassmakers' reference. The venerable glass tile maker continues the mysterious alchemies of four generations, preserving and reviving the ancient Byzantine craft of gold leaf mosaic and pure enamels of Murano's Renaissance. Orsoni continues as guardian of the ancient craft and creator of new materials and trends in the mosaic arts.
Photo courtesy Orsoni

Recent popularity has encouraged new glass technology—colors, textures, patterns, shapes, and sizes that include large-format tiles that are *au courant*.

These advancements, and tile's many virtues, make glass tile fashionable and increasingly the material of choice for uncommon design projects.

Renown designer David Easton chose glass tile for a client's New York City bathroom because it created a sense of greater spatial depth "without resorting to clichés such as mirroring." Glass tile also added a sensation of looking out of and opening up the space. "Glass tile *etherealizes* the space," says Mr. Easton.

For their many projects across the country, New York City architect Warren Bohn and his interior design partner Kelly Woodruff frequently turn to glass. "The cleanliness and clarity of the surface, as well as its easy maintenance makes it ideal for use in many applications, but especially in baths," says Mr. Woodruff, whose work is shown in Figure 131.

Architect turned fashion designer Gianfranco Ferré turned to glass tile in his design of a shower for his urban day spa, *E'Spa at Gianfranco Ferré* in Milan. Ferré pitted gloriously luminous 24-karat gold mosaic tiles against dark, rich metallic-looking mosaics custom-colored for him by Bisazza. The sensational effect can be seen in Figures 35a-35b. He says, "Now I go to the very origin of utter luminosity which becomes a visual, sensorial pleasure."

Marcel Wanders, a leading *tres avant garde* European designer, designed and executed in glass mosaic an overscaled textile pattern that covers a long bathroom bench, which can double as a counter. It fits beneath the sloped ceiling of a suite he designed in Amsterdam. The smooth tiled white bench contrasts with the soft dark brown of the wooden ceiling in a simple monochromatic scheme. It relates harmoniously with luxurious linens and compatibly tinted bath tiles in a minimalist style that speaks of comfort and convenience without fussiness or pretension. See this room in Figure 133a.

Designer Marc Thee of Marc-Michaels Designs in Florida, and one of *Architectural Digest's* perennial *Top 100 Designers*, finds glass tile appropriate for elegant, essentially traditional interiors all through the house. See his work in Chapter One.

For a new kitchen design, noted South Florida designer Alan Cohen of Cohen Geller Associates chose glass tile to reference his client's growing collection of *Art Deco* glass. See this kitchen in Figure 72.

Designers Robert Reid and Darin Brooks of brooks • reid studio in Houston, chose mosaic glass tile for a remodeled 1950s bathroom because it suited their "sculptured wall" design. The designs call for tile to look like a textile sheet "rolling down the wall." The terminating outward curve fills a three-inch gap between the wall and existing terrazzo floor that was created when the old vanity was removed. The designers note that sometimes, necessity prompts an unusually clever and effective design. "Using a small-scale mosaic glass tile gave us the opportunity to create a three-dimensional textural quality to the wall and a depth that cannot be achieved with a glazed tile," says Mr. Reid. Clients tell him that now, instead of congregating in the kitchen, guests congregate around this newly renovated *feature* room (Figure 48).

If these busy professional designers' appreciation of glass tile is a true indicator, the history of glass tile will continue to unfold as more and more lovers of beauty discover unique glass tile in our books and in showrooms everywhere.

To make a mosaic, you have to think mosaic ... it can't be done in any other way. The purity of a line is a sort of musical line. If I had to define my mosaic, I would call it a mosaic score.

—*Maestro Lucio Orsoni*

Chapter 1
Glass Tile Style for Home and Garden

The magic of glass—dancing light, sparkling color, sheer beauty, excellent performance—right for every style

Looking for glass tile to suit a particular decorating style or project? It's out there! As interiors and tiles throughout this book show, there is a glass tile for every taste.

With the gazillions of glass tiles—in a staggering array of colors, patterns, finishes, textures, sizes, and shapes—all it takes is time and stamina to find the *just-right* tile. Lucky searchers will find a showroom nearby as wonderful as Alan Court's heart-of-the-village shop in East Hampton, New York, where on weekends practically everyone on the street is an international celebrity. Here are choices in glass tile to satisfy the most discriminating tastes.

If, for any reason, the tile needed for a particular project does not exist, then some company specializing in custom tile will make it! Oceanside Glasstile matched a *fleck* of red found in an existing terrazo floor for a brooks. reid studio project! See it in Figure 48. KOG has been creating special colors for unique projects for many years. Marin Designworks, Orsoni, Bisazza, and perhaps most manufacturers do this. It's a good idea to ask.

Just as color-matching is not a problem for many, certain companies also make special sizes and shapes. See Chapter Seven, Sources, for contact information for all of the firms whose materials are shown in *Designing and Living With Glass Tile*. For inspiration for projects that will enhance your own home and garden, read on.

All Through the House

Speaking poetically, all glass tile *dances* with the light.

Glass tile refracts light: grasps, bends, twists, flexes, shapes, and sends light back into the room. All this animation makes lively glass tile shimmer, glimmer, gleam, glow, sparkle, and shine. These elegant qualities are appropriate for the formal, dressy, chic interiors found in many different historic decorating styles and periods. And, they work in some contemporary interiors!

For more casual styles, special finishes create a softer matte surface. Consider tile with a matte finish for a lakeside or beach house, a rustic lodge look, or country style.

Texture—smooth, polished, embossed, tumbled—also affects how a glass tile works with a certain decorating scheme. Many choices in textures make it easy to design custom interiors and to create truly personal style.

Style — *Traditional*

Old World elegance is evident in Marc-Michaels' entry hall with its spiraling staircase, glass-walled dining room, beamed-ceiling kitchen, and barrel-vaulted bathroom. Glass tile is at home in this grandeur. In the hands of the gifted Marc Thee, a principal in Marc-Michels, glass tile is treated as a precious gem. See his deft use of glass mosaic in the circular floor medallion in this entry hall, the spill-proof dining room floor, the magnificent kitchen hood, and the glorious bathroom ceiling (Figures 2-5).

Figure 2. Glass tiles in the decorative floor medallion add a deft touch of refined sparkle to a formal entry by Marc-Michaels Interior Design.
Photo by Sargent Architectural Photography, courtesy Marc-Michaels Interior Design

Figure 4. Interior designer Marc Thee of Marc-Michaels Interior Design integrates a sleek stainless steel hood into an eclectic kitchen with Moorish accents by cleverly surrounding the hood with a smart background and border of glass mosaic tile. The result—a design whose elements sing in perfect harmony.
Photo by Sargent Architectural Photography, courtesy Marc-Michaels Interior Design

Figure 5. For an ethereal effect, Interior Designer Marc Thee clads a barrel vaulted ceiling in a gradient blend of water-color tinted mosaic glass tiles. Ceiling tiles are a soft counterpoint to other light-reflecting surfaces in this master bath that include glass, mirror, and polished stone.
Photo by Sargent Architectural Photography, courtesy Marc-Michaels Interior Design

Figure 3. (opposite) Glass tile borders add discreet pattern interest and textural counterpoint that fashionably update the elegant floor in a gracious formal Florida dining room designed by Marc-Michaels Interior Design.
Photo by Sargent Architectural Photography, courtesy Marc-Michaels Interior Design

Style — *Contemporary*

Glass tile is always *au courant*. There is nothing old-fashioned about glass tile mosaic, and larger format glass tile is definitely current. In contemporary interiors, glass tile may star, or be completely integral as it is in the living room and home office shown in Figures 6a-6b. In each, walls wearing Trend's Liberty collection in Lalique blue, appear atmospheric. As this shimmering cool color appears to dance away, glass tile walls seem as un-confining as the adjoining clear glass wall with its endless-horizon view.

Glass tile is versatile. See it in all its forms in interiors of many different styles throughout *Designing and Living With Glass Tile*. Art Deco, Southwestern, lakeside cottage, Colorado contemporary, Miami condominium, and more are featured and all are sources of inspiration.

Tile for Every Space

After seeing Marc-Michaels' traditional style entry and dining room, and Trend's contemporary style living room and home office, it is obvious that there is a glass tile that is right for all styles and for *every room*. In short, to see it is to realize that glass tile is not for kitchens and baths *only*.

Other living and live-in rooms suitable for glass tile include a modern media room inspired by Japanese residential architecture. This room is the creation of Jordan Goldstein, AIA, and Jill Goebel, IIDA, both of Gensler, the nation's leading architectural firm. Goldstein is a principal in the company's Washington, DC, office. We might call this media room Romantic Modern, since it combines visual poetry with state-of-the-art technology. Glass tile's luminous beauty and technical aspects contributes to both (Figures 114-116).

Bedrooms are appropriate places for glass tile. The designer of a bedroom in Domus Orsoni designed a gorgeous glass tile headboard with 24-karat gold to match that of walls in an adjoining bathroom. The villa, the childhood home of Lucio Orsoni, a descendant of company founder Angelo Orsoni, is now a guesthouse for company visitors. Other bedrooms from this glorious villa are shown in this book. They include the "Love" bedroom (Figure 34a) and a mysterious dark-walled bedroom with a Sicis Glimmer glass headboard. Backlit, it glows in the dark; it glows naturally in daylight.

Of course kitchens are just the place for glass tile. A smorgasbord of designs in the book range from city-slick to lakeside estate-style, to San Francisco Bay area sophisticate, and more. Enjoy!

Bathrooms and glass tile are great go-togethers. Name your style: Paris garret, toney East Hampton country house, urbane, suburban, Italian baroque, or country rustic. You will find them all in this book.

Name your mood—glass tile will interpret it: Chi-chi, chic, glamorous, funky, casual, elegant, dressy, formal, and laid back (literally, in the spas in Figures 91 and 99).

Figures 6a-6b. (above and opposite) In a living room and home office, Trend's Liberty collection glass tile in Lalique blue emphasizes the elements of light and air, essential components of contemporary interior design. The Liberty Collection by Giulio Candussio utilizes the transparency of glass to create a balance of essential shapes, modular rhythms, and color. The result, Candussio says, is a continuous and changing bright and chromatic vibration that comes from the surface itself.
Photo courtesy Trend

Figure 7. Architect Fabio Rotella chose Orsoni 24-karat gold and turquoise tessera for a unique contemporary-style headboard he designed for a guestroom at Domus Orsoni in Venice. The elegant villa was the childhood home of master mosaic artist Lucio Orsoni, whose great-grandfather Angelo founded the famed Angelo Orsoni Mosaici company.
Photo by Arnaldo Dal Bosco, courtesy Orsoni

Figure 8. Designer Marco Nereo Rotelli writes glowingly in Orsoni gold mosaic in his romantic *Stones of Venice* guest bedroom at Domus Orsoni.
Photo courtesy Orsoni

Tile as Focal Point

Ask any designer—the fireplace is the *must-have* focal point for every room. And fascinating glass tile is the material of choice for boosting the allure of the fire. We show you several, beginning on page 13, and there are others throughout the book.

Tile as Decorative Accessory

Designers find many places for tile other than walls, floors, and ceilings. See a number of ideas throughout these pages, including covering plastic cubes with glass tile and backlighting them for the most romantic of bedrooms (Figure 62).

Tile on a Budget, and Other Decorating Ideas

A discreet use of tile—because a little is all a project needs, or the budget is small—can be a very effective decorating decision. Here are some suggestions:

- Create a chair-rail for the dining room or kitchen
- Cover just the wainscot area (space below a chair rail) in glass tile—plain, patterned, or textured
- Frame a frameless mirror in a bathroom or hallway
- Cover window reveals (space between window glass and wall)
- Transform a closet into a bar (remove the door, glass-tile the walls, add clear glass shelves
- Surround wall sconces and chandeliers with glass tile plaques—round, square, diamond, or dog-eared shaped
- Cover clear plastic cubes with transparent glass tile and backlight, or cover a melamine cube with opaque glass tile for the beach house
- Create a headboard of translucent glass tile and backlight, or cover an existing headboard with iridescent tiles
- Highlight a niche by covering the walls inside with glass tile in a stand-out bright or color of choice
- Glamorize a simple bench by covering it in glass tile
- Create an art object—inspired by the one in Figure 35a—by covering a ball or box form in glass tile
- Cover a focal wall in glass tile of choice

Fireplaces, Natural Focal Points

A fireplace in any room is the primary focal point.

A glowing fireplace—the traditional symbol of home—is a source of infinite fascination. Capturing every play of flickering light emanating from the hearth, as glass tile does, makes the fireplace an even stronger focal point day and night, year in, year out.

Design treatments for fireplace façades are essentially decorative. The abundance of tile colors, finishes, textures, and patterns in glass tile allows for creative expression. Remarkably, there is a glass tile for every recognized interior design style and period. With the abundance of tiles, there is also unlimited possibility for personal expression.

For the adventurous designer, tiles offer inexhaustible possibilities for expressing personal moods, visions, and whimsies—however improbable or unexpected. A case in point is Mixed-Up Mosaic's *Home Feet Home* fireplace that pairs a happy-go-lucky barefoot motif surround and hearth with a formal French mantel.

Crossville's brilliant green *Illuminessence* tiles for raised hearth, surround, and mantel add elegance to the fireplace's Craftsman-style simplicity. There's a sense of infinite satisfaction in the interplay between the simple geometry of square tiles along the hearth and diamond-shaped tiles that march across the mantel front. And the color is superb.

A little glass tile can have enormous impact. Marblized glass tile by the former Louis Comfort Tiffany & Company supplier, Kokomo Opalescent Glass Tile (KOB), is the ideal frame for the opening of one fireplace with a simple Georgian mantel—a discreet but highly effective touch. For another, decorative inserts from Boyce and Bean provide both a focal point above the grate and a frame on either side that keep the fireplace interesting – even when there is no fire.

When a design is pared down to a few essential lines, in the Modern mode, elegantly simple iridescent mosaic glass tiles provide arresting visual interest. Add to the iridescence a powerful color as in Oceanside's tile and the design is complete, whether the fireplace is in a thoroughly modern or more rustic room. Lighter, brighter glass tiles by Erin Adams (from Ann Sacks) blend beautifully with simple, modern styling—adding unobtrusive elegance.

Glass tile comes in a wide assortment of sizes and

The first piece of furniture for every living room is a fireplace.

—*David Easton, Interior Designer*

Figure 9. Gold mirror mini-mosaic—smaller than 1x1-inch pieces—cover a curvilinear fireplace with dazzling splendor. Any fireplace is the memory-making focal point of any room. This one is unforgettable.
Photo courtesy Mixed-Up-Mosaics

Figure 10. Tiles from Crossville's Illuminessence Glass Collection surround the fireplace, lighting up the room day and night. Designed by venerable glass tile maker Boyce & Bean, tiles are made of cast, translucent glass that is textured front and back. These tiles in a wide color range are designed to capture, refract, bend, and twist light in a never-ending light show.
Photo courtesy Crossville, Inc.

shapes, including bricks ranging from a regular size and shape to mini bricks and slender bricks. Mixed-Up Mosaics successfully combines mostly-red skinny brick shaped tiles as a cover-up for a simple fireplace that sets atop a raised marble hearth. As a finishing touch, a glass-tile framed mirror hangs above the mantel.

For sheer glamour, the most extravagant expression in glass tile is the design that utilizes 24-karat gold mosaic tesserae. Gold tesserae are ablaze with light even when there is no fire!

No matter what the style—elegant or rustic, formal or relaxed, grand or whimsical—glass tile hearths, surrounds, and mantels extend the brilliance and beauty of fire.

Figure 11. An elegantly simple traditional style fireplace puts on a fashionable face when updated with glass tile. The company recommends the use Boyce & Bean's Water & Light Collection in a single finish—clear, frosted, or iridescent—or in a combination of finishes. Or, for maximum light play, they suggest using the Dichro Moon Glass Collection. Any—and all—of these glass tile collections are designed to make the most of ambient and fire light.
Photo courtesy Boyce & Bean Natural Glass & Clay Co.

Figure 12. Designer Andy Marcus, president of ALM Interior Design, resurfaced the 15-foot high cinderblock fireplace in his Palm Springs home with Hakatai's Ashland Series glass tile, creating a spectacular focal point that updates the entire house.
Photo courtesy Hakatai Enterprises

Figures 12a-12b. Interior Designer Vivian Dowsett's client asked for something "bright and fun" for a new fireplace surround. Ms. Dowsett (collaborating with Lea Wynn of Durrant & Assoc., Salt Lake City, Utah) chose sparkling glass tile from the Crystal Visions Collection(TM). Designed by Barbara J. Cashman for GlasTile Inc., handmade fused-glass tiles in different colors are backed with a clear mirror that is cut to size and hand-applied to individual tiles. Ms. Dowsett says the tiles complement both her client's personality and artwork.
Photo courtesy GlasTile Inc.

In the Garden

If your garden isn't magic, add glass tile. The interplay of light with glass will charm even the birds and bees.

Begin with the garden wall: On the exterior and near the gate, a fanciful glass tile creature like Faducci's leaping-lizards tree frog could greet all comers. Its "ready to spring over the garden wall" posture encourages entry! Its eager agility challenges. Its beautiful tactile surface invites a pat and suggests camaraderie. It's an instant pet!

Dress up the inside wall, as mosaic artist Mariel Hautoux did a lanai in Miami. Walls meant to confine, need not be stifling. The large-scale design by Ms. Hautoux captures the eye and incites the imagination. The interplay between the design and the garden keeps the eye moving, heightening the experience of being in the garden and moving through the space—even while standing or sitting in one spot. Such a design in shimmering glass tile is sheer magic.

Planter gardens are all the rage—in or out of the garden. Colorful glass tile planters showcase blossoms. A great garden deserves accents like the planters by Mixed-Up-Mosaics. They engage the eye, the light, and the spirit. Large round built-ins or standing pots? Create a tableau by gathering several different sizes and shapes, and mix colors as you would a bouquet.

All gardens—especially those with beautiful leafy bowers—need a bench. One that is long enough for two with time for a chat or just soaking up the views is ideal. While any port in a storm (or bench to the fatigued) is good, a *beautiful* port—like Hidden Springs Designs' garden bench—becomes a destination (especially on a sunny day).

A table is a natural companion to a bench, and a good place for parking a beverage, book, or a trowel. It makes having a picnic in the garden easy to arrange, even at the spur of the moment. Mixed-Up-Mosaics table mixes tiles in summer-flower-garden colors. Unlike flowers, these colorful table tiles will not fade, neither will they wilt! Since glass is water- and stain-proof, there's no need to fret. Probably a hosing from time to time will keep such a table in tip-top shape, ready for *impromptu* tea parties.

Pools are very much a part of today's gardens. In fact, often they take up the lion's share of garden space. Nearby, for convenience, often is an outdoor kitchen under a protective porch or patio roof (Figure 28).

A great *unifying* decorating idea is to create an outdoor kitchen backsplash of glass tile to match that in the nearby pool. Designers did that for the Builder's House, an annual showcase of the National Association of Home Builder's forward-looking design-build concepts. For a gracious Old World Style house in Orlando, Florida, Crossville glass tile in a brilliant blue adorns the patio kitchen wall and the close-by, stunningly beautiful undulating pool.

Pools with blue glass tile liners sparkle plenty, even as they blend with sky. A good design idea is to add a decorative fountain at the far end of a long pool. This is the spot where the eye wishes to see decorations as playful and witty as those by Mariel Hautoux (Figures 23a-23c).

Fountains need not be huge to satisfy a longing to hear the soothing sounds of splashing water in a garden. A small fountain tucked into the corner of the wall (Figure 24) delivers a beautiful sight and musical sound in great style.

At many homes, the pool is a destination. One look is to love the shimmer and shine of gorgeous glass tile that lines a pool and pool surround. With or without pattern, a pool lined in translucent, opaque, or iridescent glass tiles like the Crossville tiles in the Builder's House pool,

Figure 13. Frost-resistant art for the garden by mosaic artists Solomon Bassoff and Domenica Motarella of Faducci, LLC, is inspired by nature. Made of hand-sculpted cement over a steel armature that is painstakingly covered in glass mosaic; their magical creatures come to life as fierce-looking Komodo dragons, marine iguanas, dogs (sometimes with wings), or other animals. Here, a climbing frog that graces a garden wall can also come in out of the cold and with equal ease adorn an indoor wall.
Photo by Orin Bassoff, courtesy Faducci

is endlessly intriguing.

While beautifully designed pools are destinations, they are also points of departure for the imagination. Even a glimpse of dreamy pools like those shown here is transporting.

An outdoor shower between pool and house (or house and beach, if one is so lucky) is a fun place to wash off—especially when splash-proof walls wear mosaic glass tile in patterns that mimic the garden. Of course, the oversized scale of the flowers in a design by Mariel Hautoux executed in tiles by Trend, adds to the feeling of fun and frolic.

Glass tile and gardens go together—naturally.

Figure 15. A mosaic-covered sneaker! If not for the garden itself, then for the patio, terrace, or porch wall that cries out for witty art that will carry on a dialogue with both candle- and sunlight.
Photo courtesy Mixed-Up-Mosaics

Figure 14. Mosaic artist Mariel Hautoux, president of Art & Maison Miami, created the captivating, undulating glass mosaic mural that adds color, pattern, and texture to enliven the wall of an enclosed lanai.
Photo by Sergio Fama, courtesy Art & Maison Miami

Figure 16. An outdoor shower in Coral Gables, Florida, bares glorious Enamels glass tessera from Orson to exuberantly rival the beauty of live orchids.
Photo courtesy Orsoni

Figure 17. A garden bench flowers into an art object in the hands of mosaic artists Rob Matthews and Leslie Guinan of Hidden Springs Designs. Tucked into a cozy niche and surrounded by fragrant foliage, such a bench becomes a much-visited destination.
Photo courtesy Hidden Springs Designs

Figures 18a-18c. Sparkling colorful glass mosaic planters and tabletops are to a garden what bouquets of wonderful flowers are to a room!
Photos courtesy Mixed-Up-Mosaics

Figures 19a-19b-19c. A key living area in some climates, the great outdoor kitchen can be just as dressed up as the living room. Here, Crossville's Glass Blox Collection brings shimmering color to the backsplash, a brilliant counterpoint to stainless steel cabinetry and appliances. Nearby is the romantic, meandering courtyard pool lined in tile from the same collection. This Old World style home in Orlando, Florida, showcases the talents of the National Association of Homebuilders.
Photography by James F. Wilson, courtesy Crossville
(Read more about this uniquely color coordinated collection in Chapter Two, Color.)

Figure 20. Garden themes inspire mosaic artist Jenny Perry, who may render koi swimming in a birdbath, or depict a busy bee hovering above pollen-laden flowers, perfectly capturing the ideal summer day. Jenny's busy bee mural is created with Bisazza, Opio, and Kaleidoscope tiles.
Photo courtesy Originally Jenny Mosaics

Figure 21. A glass leaf "tile" by mosaic artist Lynn Moor would be at home indoors or out —perhaps on a patio wall—and beautifully reflects the urge to unite house and garden.
Photo courtesy Lynn Moor

Figure 22. Mosaic artist Julie Richey's orchard-inspired Apples—a fine-art work to be savored—are the perfect accent to an outdoor or indoor kitchen.
Photo by Stacy Dail Bratton Photography, courtesy Julie Richey Mosaics

Figures 23a-23c. A fountain becomes a work of art and scenic backdrop for an outdoor pool in the expert hands of mosaic artist Mariet Hautoux, who embellishes the surface with fanciful wading birds, seahorses, fish, scrolls, and other delightful images in glass tile.
Photo by Sergio Fama, courtesy Art & Maison Miami

Figure 24. A unique corner fountain in the Palm Springs, California, home of Designer Andy Marcus is clad in Hakatai's Ashland Series glass tile with rough-cut edges and random crazing that gives it a handmade look. The tile, in the Clear Ice colorway, has a liquid look and lively sparkle that rivals that of flowing water.
Photo courtesy Hakatai Enterprises

Figure 25. Ibarra Rosano Design Architects chose Hakatai's Carter Series glass mosaic tile for the perimeter and vertical walls of the Winter/Rosenfield ranch home in Tucson. The Light Denim color complements both water and sky.
Photo courtesy Hakatai Enterprises

Figure 26. Aureo glass tile by Trend sandwiches 24-karat gold leaf between clear glass and brilliantly refracts and interacts with the bright summer sky—a continual light show.
Photo courtesy Trend

Figure 27. A wading pool and spa get the same glamour treatment as the accompanying regulation pool—surfaces of dazzling glass mosaic tile—by mosaic artist Mariel Hautoux.
Photo by Sergio Fama, courtesy Art & Maison Miami

Chapter 2
Color

Magical color creates dazzling feats of illusion.

Color (and especially colorful *pattern*) disguises boundaries established by Line. Call this the camouflage principle.

For example, generally light colors make rooms look larger. But many designers use dark color in a small room to make the lines that mark corners (and join wall to ceiling) *invisible* (seem to fade from view), and thus the room seems larger. Color a high, unattractive restaurant ceiling black and *presto,* it disappears from view. Rich warm color pulls a too-high ceiling down. Light (not stark-contrast white) color pushes a too-low ceiling up, up, and away. Rich warm colors pull distant walls closer, while light cool colors distance too-near walls, creating a sense of spaciousness. Call it remodeling with color magic.

Colorful glass tile—with its refractive, light-reflecting qualities and liquid pool-like depth—makes walls seem to dance, float, and do just about anything but simply stand there.

Beautifully colored glass tile performs many illusions as it refracts, reflects, bends, twists, shimmers, glimmers, and sparkles in an endless dance with light, Interaction with light gives glass its luminous glow and sense of depth—a great relief from confining flat, matte walls. Fine artists call this "piercing the plane"—encouraging one to believe it possible to see beyond the surface. Paint tries to do this with glazing. Natural stone attempts it with a high, light-reflecting polish. Glass tile does it naturally.

Color is affected by finish and texture (see Chapter Four). Iridescence, an example of surface-changing finish, fascinates with its constantly shifting color that creates a perpetual light-and-color show. And precious metals—24-karat white and yellow gold and others—sandwiched between crystal clear glass—add exciting finish. Textural interest joins with color to provide even more arresting looks to capture attention.

Altogether, tile's amazing color story is enhanced by a vast number of finishes, textures, patterns, sizes, and shapes.

Choosing Color

There is a lot to consider in selecting color for a glass tile project. To smooth the process, basically there are two methods: objective and subjective.

The objective—favored by professional designers—takes a problem/solution approach. It assumes that problems can be defined and solutions provided.

The subjective, very personal approach assumes that one knows what one likes—friends and neighbors, problems/solutions, and decorating rules be hanged.

Here is a brief look at both.

Choosing Color Objectively

This approach demands a cool head and unswerving eye—a "what's wrong with this space" critique. After defining the problems, the next step is to arrive at a solution. This is more easily done using tried-and-true decorating rules that address the problem and offer a rational solution.

For example, a problem kitchen is a long rectangle with a dark far wall. This is an awkward and uninviting space. The decorating rule says that a strong warm color will make the far wall appear to advance and the room seem more cheerful.

The choice of *which* warm color among a dozen suitable tones may be objective (X, slightly grayed, works better than Y, which is a little too bright); or, subjective and very personal (I *like* this red tone best).

There are many real problems that color can solve and we list some in "Common Problems/Solutions. (For more about color rules that apply to problems and solutions, see our *Home Decorating for Dummies*.)

Selecting Color Subjectively

The *purely personal* approach to choosing color involves the heart, not the head, so it is a no-brainer—but not without consequences. That is, loving a light, cool color is easy. But choosing one to make a distant wall in a long, rectangular room appear to come closer and the room look cozier is not in the cards!

Another strong argument against opting for just any color that appeals is that it may not appeal to a potential owner at resale time.

Those two well-known arguments aside, selecting colored tile subjectively should be a truly custom approach that considers many personal points. The key to color happiness will be in following Shakespeare's dictum: To thine own self be true. Here are some "know thyself" basics:

- **Flattering color**. Are you blonde, brunette, redhead? Walls, floor, and ceiling color (especially in bedrooms) should be keyed to your personal coloring and create a flattering background. The room is the stage; you are the star. Consider making a ceiling a "never need a facelift" pink or pinky red that flatters (Figure 56).
- **Emotional well-being color**. Color affects and effects emotion. Do you like to wake up slowly and drift gently into the day? Choose a gentle, atmospheric color—cooler or warmer, a personal preference. Do you want an eye-opening, catapulting color that starts you and your day in high gear—something hot, say hot pink, red, or orange? Do you need intense, peppy color to perk you up (perhaps a sunny yellow); or soothing colors that let you slip into the day? Are warm colors that welcome you home, or safe-haven hues that help you wind down after a chaotic day the ticket to a pleasing color scheme?
- **Mono or more color scheme?** Since color is stimulating, you will need to know whether "a" or "b" applies.
  - a) *Less is more color.* Choose a simple, one-color scheme to satisfy your need for order, calm, and clarity.
  - b) *Too much-is-never-enough color*. A multi-colored or a crazy-quilt color scheme should satisfy the too-much-is-never-enough motto that our favorite architect, the late Morris Lapidus, espoused and you embrace.
- **Stimulus boundaries**. In addition to how many colors, the question is how much color do you personally prefer? Will you need a lot of wow color—say four walls? Or, will a little dab do—a focal wall?
- **Personal style**. Your style may be entirely personal (eclectic or beyond). Or, you may just put your personal stamp on some historic, traditional or other style, updating it in the process. In any case, color choice is an opportunity to bring a vague vision into sharp, realized focus.

All colors—including the metallics, reds, pinks, blues, greens, warm neutrals, and cool neutrals that follow—are enormously versatile and inspirational, whether chosen objectively or subjectively!

Common Problems/Solutions

To get the most from color, know what task you want to perform! In a nutshell:

- ***Create a mood**. Youthful—choose primary colors. Adult—choose secondary colors. Warm—choose colors on the warm side of the color wheel. Cool—stick to colors on the cool side of the color wheel. Cheerful—yellows are tried-and-true sunshine colors.*
- ***Create a style**. Formal—secondary or tertiary colors suit this dressy look. Casual—earthy colors work. Modern—super cools are true to form. Contemporary—brights add currency.*
- ***Direct traffic.** Strong, bright, and warm colors pull the eye and the body follows.*
- ***Furnish a sparse space**. Color enriches and colorful pattern furnishes—especially small hallways and rooms with little floor space.*
- ***Reshape space**. Call it remodeling with color. Use these color powers to work to re-do space without hammer or nails: visually eliminate confining lines, direct traffic, raise and lower ceilings, move walls closer or further away, add or subtract weight (darker shades are "heavier"), and so forth, as mentioned above.*

Tip: The key to Personal Style—and choosing color to express it—is to "know thyself," and to thine own vision be true!

Tip: Brilliant colors seem more brilliant in contrast to more modest, less flamboyant colors placed next to them.

Tip: Color is effective, even when used in restraint (small amount).

Coloring Tile

Glass tiles are colored in different ways that may affect their performance. For a full discussion, see our Glass Tile Inspirations for Kitchens and Baths, *Schiffer Publishing. Here, briefly, are the three key ways in which color is added to glass tile.*

- Cast glass has coloring agents added to the mix during the manufacturing process so that it is integral and cannot fade or deteriorate.
- Fused glass sandwiches color between layers of clear glass which bonds (fuses) molecularly under super high heat. These colors, too, do not fade or deteriorate.
- Enameled glass color is painted onto the backside of glass. It is extremely important that this color not be exposed to moisture or chemicals that would degrade the color, which is also susceptible to UV rays.

Figure 29. Angelo Orsoni opened the doors to his glass foundry in 1888, and has been producing extraordinarily colored tessera ever since—some from ancient and others from new formula. The Orsoni color library is extensive!
Photo courtesy Orsoni

Figure 30. Erin Adams' Quilt pattern fuses layers of beautifully contrasting color in a tile with a gently pillowed top.
Photo courtesy Erin Adams

Tip: Energize a room design by contrasting cool vs. warm or light vs. dark colors.

Figure 31. The Paragon Series from Country Floors offers the interior designer options in a broad spectrum of brilliant colors, ranging from pastels to jewel-tones (5_10), and clear, clear with copper foil or white backing, frosted, and iridescent finishes.
Photo courtesy Country Floors

Figure 32. Sicis' Glimmer collection, a transparent glass with a luxurious mother-of-pearl iridescent finish, is available in twenty-nine colors, suitable for indoor and outdoor installation.
Photo courtesy Sicis

Metallics

Figure 33. A vivid barrel vaulted ceiling reigns over a floor of glass tiles from Bisazza's Oro Pavimento collection which features hand-applied 24-karat gold leaf sandwiched between two layers of glass. Tiles are hand-cut to required sizes in 20mm or 10mm squares and are available in smooth or wavy surface finishes. Tall lacquered doors, a gold-leafed screen behind dark wood chairs, and a gold-leafed side table underscore an atmosphere of ultimate luxury. *Photo by Paolo di Pietri, courtesy Bisazza*

Metallics bring the unique colors and high reflectivity of precious gold, silver, and copper to glass tile—a marriage made in creative heaven. The result, when used to cover large spaces, is a look of ultra luxury. Used discreetly, even a small amount of metallic glass tile—a "fine art" piece, backsplash, or focal wall—adds gleam that brightens gloomy spaces.

Manufacturing techniques for these often pricey collections vary from company to company, and from collection to collection. To be sure, proprietary manufacturing methods are as carefully guarded as state secrets. What manufacturers do tell us about their collections is helpful in selecting tile.

Bisazza's Oro Collection—the company's most opulent tile product—is a composition of hand-applied 24-karat gold leaf "sandwiched" between two layers of glass. Each fragment is meticulously hand-cut to the required size. This super-luxe tile is available as Rivestimento for walls and Pavimento for floors, and are available in 20mm or 10mm squares and in a smooth or wavy finish.

Bisazza's Oro BIS collections also consist of a "sandwich of gold." That is, each pricey tile has hand-applied 24-karat gold leaf between two layers of glass. But, this collection differs from Oro in that "a new manufacturing process" yields tessera that are perfectly square, with a consistent thickness, and beveled edges. They are exactly the same as 20x20 and 10x10 mm tiles in the company's Mosaic collection, which means that tiles from these two collections can be intermingled.

Designers Love Gold

Gold—in its traditional yellow color, adds warmth to all styles, and is especially compatible with traditional, and eclectic styles that update traditional interiors.

Figures 34a-34b. Marco Nereo Rotelli, designer of the "Stones of Venice" bedroom at the Domus Orsoni in Venice, was inspired by Ruskin's "The Stone of Venice." So, he created a little room that contains big words—a little *bright* room, he says, that leads to splendor and means to inspire dreams. Rotelli believes that words change the world. He wonders what dreams other bedrooms inspire.
Photograph by Arnaldo dal Bosco, interior design by Marco Nereo Rotelli, courtesy Trend

Figures 35a-35b. Here are interior design ideas for luxury home spas from Gianfranco Ferre's E'ESPA in Milan. Cover walls with glass tiles flecked with 24-karat gold and highlight the shower with 24-karat gold leaf tiles from Bisazza's Oro collection. In a niche, add one important piece of fine art, like the golden globe resting on a rare-marble base in a meditation and resting area. *Photo courtesy Bisazza*

Figure 36. OriginalStyle mixes metals by surrounding a gold-look square with copper in its Phoebus and Gold tile from the Float-and-Foil Metallics collection. Combine these highly decorative tiles for all out wow power, drop into other field tile as decorative accents, or create a border.
Photo courtesy OriginalStyle

Gold is timeless

Yellow gold is classic, timeless. Noted mosaic artist Lynn Moor continues the great fine-art tradition begun by artists who incorporated gold mosaic in their murals for great cathedral murals like that at St. Mark's (San Marco) in Venice (Figure 38). But, in a more contemporary vein, her work departs from figurative subjects to become a study in two vital elements of classic design—balance and rhythm.

Eclectic interior design relies on those and other classic elements to mix ancient and modern furnishings. Classic elements in both make it possible to successfully place modern furniture against a background of classic-looking gold glass mosaic in an updated-but-timeless over-sized, stylized, floral pattern based on an antique floral fabric.

Figure 37. To create this work of fine art, mosaic artist Lynn Moor used seventeen different shades and types of gold mosaic from Orsoni. Included are smooth and luminous tessera in white through citron, rose, and various copper golds, together with textured 24-karat bright gold. It hangs in the living room of a collector in Massachusetts.
Photo courtesy Lynn Moor

Figure 38. Seventeenth century murals above the entry to San Marco cathedral built in the ninth century in Venice are splendid in gold mosaic. Orsoni does the restoration work on murals throughout this cathedral, using 24-karat gold mosaic made to match the original colors.
Photo courtesy Orsoni

Figure 39. The dazzling gold Damasco Bianco Oro design by Carlo Dal Bianco is a larger-than-life computer-generated pattern inspired by baroque Damascus textiles that used silver and gold threads extensively. Bisazza's Oro tile collection sandwiches 24-karat gold leaf between layers of glass and is available as Rivestimento for walls and Pavimento for floors. Here, with Eero Saarinen's tulip chair and table, Damasco Bianco Oro adds hip pizzazz that updates Palazzo Style.
Photo by Federico Cedrone, Styling Beatrice Rosetti, Credit Christofle, Il Centrotavola, Venini, Courtesy Bisazza

Trend's Aureo collection is an elegant hand-made tile with 24-karat yellow and white gold. World-renowned mosaic artist, Lucio Orsoni (who inherited the Orsoni glass company founded by his great-grandfather, Angelo), designed this collection for Trend, now a sister company. For Aureo, Lucio Orsoni created twelve colors in addition to eight variations in texture and shade of yellow and white 24-karat gold. Maestro Orsoni, master artist and teacher, believes that "to live with gold is to be absorbed in a heavenly atmosphere. Nothing adapts itself better than light reflected on a gold mosaic surface." This is something the fashion industry knows well, making gold lame a classic fabric with enormous elegance. Gold and glass tile adds the same classic, fashionable sensuality to interiors. Aureo in a glistening silver look covers floors in the belvedere at the Venetian villa that houses Trend's headquarters (Figure 42).

Figure 40. Precious gold tiles from The Scent of Colours Collection by Patrizia Gucci for Trend seem like golden windows when encased by beautifully contrasting borders of glamorous glass tile. Gold casts a glorious glow whether used sparingly or with a generous hand.
Photo courtesy Trend

Figure 41. Mosaic artist Mariel Hautoux covers a swordfish form in silver-colored glass tile, creating a witty and elegant accessory for any tropics-themed interior. (When completed, this one hung in the Museum of Art in Ft. Lauderdale, Florida.)
Photo by Sergio Fama, courtesy Art & Maison Miami

White gold adds priceless style

White gold adds sophistication that updates ancient architecture. The result is a wedding of past and present, keeping old memories alive and creating new ones.

Figure 42. Atelier Mendini and Architect Veller chose Trend's Aureo 24-karat white gold leaf tiles for this interior at the Villa alle Scalette, the Trend International headquarters in Venice. Swarovski crystal inserts embellish wall tiles, which are trimmed in Trend white gold leaf mosaic and Orsoni gray. Modern Victoria and Albert chairs by Ron Arad and the Fjord hassock by Patricia Urquiola for Moroso contrast smartly with ancient architecture.
Photo courtesy Trend

"To live with gold is to be absorbed in a heavenly atmosphere."

—Lucio Orsoni, master mosaic artist

Silver looks are sophisticated

The color of silver looks smart and sophisticated. Find it in Erin Adams' Luna Collection, which marries real aluminum with glass, and in Original Style's Brushed Steel group, which works beautifully with glass. Both of these "silver colored" collections satisfy the desire to add silver to interiors throughout the house.

Figure 43. Erin Adams Luna Collection marries square or round glass inserts with *frames* of metal, including bright aluminum in three finishes—brushed, sand-blasted, and vibrated—and brass tile in four finishes—sand-brushed, green, verdigris, and brown.
Photo courtesy Erin Adams Design

Figure 44. OriginalStyle's brushed-steel look adds deft contrast to watery-green glass background tiles.
Photo courtesy OriginalStyle

Erin Adams' Luna collection is an environmentally-conscious glass and aluminum tile collection developed with Mexico-based Allumillenium Tile. It marries metals and glass. Differences and similarities in these materials are highlighted in square tiles with either square or round glass inserts in thirty-six colors. Choices of metal finishes include bright aluminum and brass. Aluminum is available in three finishes, including brushed, sand-blasted, and vibrated. The brass comes in four finishes (sand-brushed, green, verdigris, and brown). The handcrafted tiles are available in sizes ranging from 1" x 6" to 6" x 6". Both sizes and shapes can be customized to accommodate a wide range of decorative plans (Figure 43).

Figure 45. A metallic copper gleam enlivens a glass mosaic triptych that furnishes a hallway in a contemporary style home. The decidedly modern curvilinear shape of glass pieces underscore the sense of movement in a complex fine-art forest-scape by mosaic artist Erin Adams, whose unique tiles are distributed exclusively by Ann Sacks.
Photo courtesy Erin Adams Design

Mosaic tile artists seem fascinated with glass mosaic metallics. Not only does Mariel Hautoux create mosaic-patterned pools for residences and resorts, she also created "The Catch of The Day," a 6-foot tall sailfish sculpture covered in Bisazza's silver-look tile for the Museum of Art in Ft. Lauderdale, Florida. What interior designer doing a room "tropics style" wouldn't prefer the jewel-like sculpture? Her pool mermaid (Figure 146) wears a crown accented in Bisazza's gold glass mosaic.

Copper looks in glass tiles, like that in the triptych (Figure 45) by tile designer and noted artist Erin Adams, are increasingly popular. Original Style's Float & Foil Collection features copper. Occasionally, a tile appears to beautifully *combine* copper and gold, like Original Style's Phoebus and Gold tile (Figure 36).

Many other manufacturers and designers create and work with gold and other metallics. How could anyone (even wearing sunglasses) miss seeing the glorious mosaic gold-covered fireplace by Mixed-Up-Mosaics (Figure 9). To find out whether a favorite glass tile manufacturer produces a metallic collection, just check on-line. (see Chapter 7, Sources).

Figure 46. The Marquisa Satin collection by GlasTile is a satin-smooth metallic-finished tile in bronze, steel, or gold colorways, available in custom sizes or a range of stock sizes.
Photo courtesy GlasTile

Red

Red, one of the three primary colors, is the hottest color in the color spectrum, presiding over the warm side of the wheel. Memorably vivid, it symbolizes life's blood and a number of emotions, including passion, courage, aggression, and anger, as in "seeing red." It is the color of celebration and joy. It symbolizes danger and threat to life: think of stop signs, fireplugs, and small but very visible flags flying from risky cargoes traversing busy highways. It also signals help: red telephone booths, fire trucks.

Reds wear nifty names: Crimson, scarlet, rose, ruby—some the names of favorite heroines, family members, and friends.

Red is strongly identified with fruits, including strawberries, cherries, plums, apples, and watermelon. And tomatoes. There are a number of wine reds (and red wines): rose, claret, and burgundy.

Red roses are the symbol of love.

Red plays a role in fabrics, including velvet, chintz, and gingham, and canvas where it joins white to create awning stripes. Red and white toile is practically synonymous with French country style decorating.

Red is a prominent color for clothing (including red bullfighters' capes, red velvet gowns for Christmas, and red-and-white striped tee shirts for summer fun.

Red is a dominant color in many historical decorating styles, including Traditional, Victorian, Country, and Contemporary. For centuries it has been important in furnishings, and we see it in such classics as the turkey red of Oriental rugs, ruby red goblets, cranberry glass,

Tip: To successfully mix or blend reds, stick to reds with the same under tone (blue, for example, or orange or pink). This ensures that colors will blend, avoiding clashing or seeming "off."

wallpapers (with red backgrounds, or red flowers on white backgrounds), silk or velvet draperies, red-glazed ceramic vases, Chinese-red lacquered furniture, and on and on.

If it seems that we are surrounded by red, perhaps it's because we are.

Responding to Red

Colorists say that all colors elicit emotional responses. It causes respiration and pulse to rise—a condition present in flight situations. Knowing that, keep red in mind for discouraging lingering in busy small bathrooms (Figures 48, 50a, 50b, and 71).

Use red to speed traffic through a long hallway (Figure 49).

Heat up the fireplace—and make the most of flames—by covering the fireplace surround in red glass mosaic, which will reflect, refract, and engage the flame in delightful, mesmerizing conversation (Figure 47).

Because red is so visible and evokes the sensation of real warmth, it is a natural color choice for entries that emphatically say welcome. That's why a Colorado architect chose Hakatai's Crimson glass mosaic tile for the entry wall beside the striking glass door to his new home (Figure 60).

Red also increases appetite—a very good thing to keep in mind when designing a dining room. Consider adding red glass tile to the ceiling. Its reflected warm glow will make everyone look healthily "in the pink."

Figure 47. Fiery red glass tile from Crossville's Glass Blox collection covers the oversized column housing a fireplace, creating a focal point of psychological and physical warmth and an arresting artwork. (Red is striking, but there are forty-three other colors in this collection by Crossville's noted color forecaster Barbara Schirmeister.)
Photo courtesy Crossville

Figure 48. Oceanside Glastile custom-colored red glass wall tiles to match a *fleck* of red in an existing terrazzo floor—so that designers Robert Reid, ASID, and Darin Brooks, IIDA, could transform an outdated bathroom.
Photo by Kennon Evett, courtesy brooks·reid studio

Red Plus

Red—a vivacious, friendly color, is a natural choice for kitchen backsplashes (Figures 53, 54, and 55). Use it as a background, a decorative dot, or an equal checkerboard partner with black. These examples happen to focus on red and black—demonstrating the enormous versatility of these two equally strong color partners. But red, a natural star, also partners beautifully with any number of colors—sometimes any number of colors used altogether! Even then, red tends to be a dominant color—standing out in the crazy-quilt color palette of a custom bar designed by Mixed-Up-Mosaics.

Try a red with other reds, yellows, blues, or any color—even pink—that strikes your fancy during the planning/experimenting stage of design. Delightful surprises happen this way—even to professional designers!

Lastly, use as much or as little mosaic glass tile as you like. To paraphrase a much-quoted motto of our favorite architect, the late Morris Lapidus, too much of a good thing is never enough. Interpreted, that means that four walls of red glass mosaic may be perfect for transforming a tiny plain-Jane foyer into a glowing jewel-box. Pat McMillan specified a fire-engine red to move buyers cheerfully along a long, narrow, dark hallway leading from the reception area of Haviland Limoges to the company's showroom. Red proved a miracle worker. Of course, one exciting focal wall may be all that personal preference, common sense, and budget allow for a home. Let all these considerations and your own good taste be your guide.

Figure 49. For 2003 Casa Cor, Brazil's annual prestigious designer showcase house, Architect Isis Viva used vivid Red 304 glass tile by Vidrotil to energize a long hallway. Red 304 furnished it with dashing color that speeds heavy traffic cheerfully along.
Photography by Sagrilo; architecture/interior design, Isis Viva; photo courtesy Vidrotil

Figures 50a-50b. When a space the size of a shower *must be* a fully-functioning, full-service bathroom, what is a designer to do? Exactly what interior designer Leonardo Annecca did—wrap walls, floor, and ceiling in glorious glass tile that makes the miniscule space live large. Red accentuates the positively genius design solution.
Photo by HappyLivingOK, courtesy LA Designs New York Paris

Figure 51. Red clear-glass tiles send a shockwave of shimmering color across a wall of dramatic black glass tiles—the perfect backdrop for a cone-shaped pedestal lavatory.
Photo courtesy OriginalStyle

Tip: To choose "just the right" red glass mosaic, consider architectural elements such as wooden beams, stone walls or floors, cabinetry, furniture and furnishings, and natural light.

Figure 52. Sicis' Glimmer collection of transparent glass with an iridescent glow is tempting in a red as bright as Eve's apple. It is also available in twenty-eight other seductive colors (and various size mosaics, mounted on paper for easy installation).
Photo courtesy Sicis

Budget Decorating Tips

Don't let the fact that glass tile may be pricey dissuade you from including it in a decorating plan. Even a small amount of this amazing material makes a big decorating statement. Here are suggestions for charming accents of glass mosaic.

- Line the inside of a built-in niche
- Surround a doorway with a narrow border
- Frame a frameless bathroom mirror
- Place a medallion in the small entryway floor
- Add a striking glass tile border above an existing backsplash
- "Write" a lovely message in gold mosaic across a simple cube nightstand (Figure 34b).

Figure 54. Red—a pepper-upper—is so powerful that even a little dab will do! Nipping the corners of square black tiles make space for small red accents that add just the right amount of spicy red glass tile from Marin Designworks to a daring black border.
Photo courtesy Marin Designworks

Figure 55. Alternating "chess or checkers" red and black squares make an emphatic, contemporary statement punctuated and enlivened by animated light play unique to glass tile.
Photo courtesy Diamond Tech

Figure 53. A narrow white tile border punctuated with small black tiles provides sharp contrast to the crimson clear-glass tile backsplash in a daringly colored kitchen.
Photo courtesy OriginalStyle

Figure 56. Red glass mosaic adds color to the ceiling, while its refracted and reflected light add endearing warm to the entire interior. This is an especially great decorating idea for any small space, including an entry hall or bathroom ceiling.
Photo courtesy Mixed-Up-Mosaics

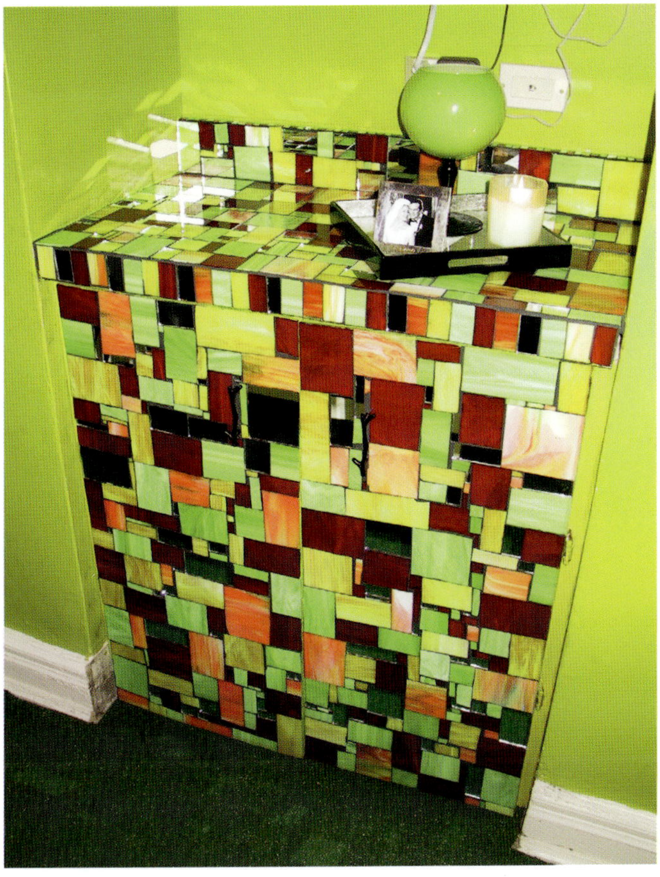

Figure 57. Red accentuates positively, energizing any color scheme. Here, red is a standout among multicolored Block Art glass tiles covering the bar area. The result is a functioning work of art that is also a focal point.
Photo courtesy Mixed-Up-Mosaics

Figure 58. Basket weave—an embossed design with bas relief motif by UltraGlas—is shown in a color at the far end of the dark red spectrum, but it is available in brighter reds (as well as thirty other standard colors). This colorway reminds designers that reds add a lively touch to blends of lighter and darker colors. Reds are especially effective when used in creating *gradients*—the random-looking mixing and mingling of many colors of small mosaic tessera.
Photo courtesy UltraGlas

Figure 59. GlasTile's red is fused (heated and bonded) into the glass so that the color will not fade nor delaminate. The red tile shown here has a distinctive stacked pattern and gently pillowed (rounded or crested) top. Look for reds also in GlasTile's Lollipop collection.
Photo courtesy GlasTile

Figure 60. From indoors and out, Hakatai's crimson red glass tile on an entry wall boldly calls attention to the eleven-foot high transparent entry door to Architect Christopher Herr's Boulder, Colorado, home. It also adds warmth so welcome on a snowy day.
Photo courtesy Hakatai Enterprises

Pink

It is impossible to think of pink without thinking of Hot Pink, the intense, saturated hue made synonymous with high fashion by fashion legend Elsa Schiaparelli. No sweet little-girl color, Hot Pink was the stuff of grown-up glamour—just the color for a clinging satin evening gown and supper at Sardi's.

A gentler, lighter pink—the color of strawberry ice cream and always accompanied by spring green—for years was *the* color for vacation homes of the rich and discreetly *un*famous—Palm Beach in winter, the Hamptons in summer. Little wonder that when all is well, we, too, say that we are in the pink!

Pink may actually be a tint of red, but such a distinct tint! It deserves its place on the warm side of the color wheel, and in the affections of those who love this color anywhere and everywhere, north, south, east, west, and all through the house. And garden—including pools, where pink adds a perky note.

In her book, *Red On Red*, Stephanie Hoppen talks about flamingo pink—redder than Hot Pink, but not red. It's an oomphy pink that pairs well with leopard prints. Although flamingo pink is much more vivid than Sicis' Glimmer pink in the dressing room in Figure 6 and bedroom in Figure 62, Glimmer pink is a decidedly sexy color that brings out the beauty in fashionable beastly leopard and zebra prints.

Mixing and Matching Pinks

Pinks mix well with other pinks—there just needs to be distinctive shifts in tints and tones for contrast. Light pinks are also great foils for reds. So, if you have been told never to use these two warm colors together, forget about it. Do use them together, especially when creating gradients or blends of glass mosaic tile for walls or floors in a room that needs to feel warm and very cozy.

Consider combining pink and red tiles together patchwork-quilt style in a Country style bathroom. Or mix pink with blue, lilac, purple or some kindred color in a crazy-quilt pattern like that in Figure 69.

Cover a column, or create a pink panel or broad decorative stripe that contrasts smartly with blue or green background tiles (Figures 63 and 66).

Use pink (one or more with one or several other colors) to create unusual stripes like those in Figure 65.

Take a cue from the designer of Orsoni's Bedford flooring (Figure 64). Give pink a more masculine air by mixing pink tile with navy blue, black, or charcoal gray. And combine pink with either subtle or vivid colors to create contemporary patterns that are both fresh and sophisticated.

Consider Pink Tile's Finish and Texture

Finish and texture will influence the selection of a particular pink glass tile for use in various rooms. Tile for a child's bathroom, for example, may be fairly simple. The fancier the finish—iridescence, for example—and the more complex the texture, the more adult-looking the tile.

Fancy finishes and textures are also suitable for sophisticated urban interiors, while tumbled, frosted, and other such surface interests will affect the selection of pink tiles for use in a country house.

Figure 61. A grown-up girl's dressing room is hot in Pink from Sicis's glamorous Glimmer collection with its dazzling iridescent finish on sparkling clear glass. A chic choice, but fashionistas will love looking at the twenty-eight other Glimmer colors (and a variety of sizes and shapes, paper mounted for easy installation).
Photo courtesy Sicis

Figure 62. Luminous night tables and a backlit headboard covered in transparent Glimmer collection mosaic glass tile from Sicis light up the night every night, and by day add a rosy glow. The tables and matching headboard are a decorating idea worth emulating.
Photo courtesy Sicis

Figure 63. Pink plus red in a wonderfully warm blend of mosaic glass tile from OriginalStyle is a fashion statement to make the heart beat faster and heat up any room. There are, of course, other choices, but pink is a perennial favorite that has never been more *en vogue*.
Photo courtesy OriginalStyle

Figure 64. Orsoni artists designed ten dramatically different patterns based on fabrics for its Tessuti di Smalto flooring collection. Tiles from the Aureo and Smalti Veneziani collections were incorporated. Bedford, shown here, combines dominant pink with black, lilac, and pale gray from the Smalti Veneziani collection. Other designers may choose from a wide array of colors in designing their own custom floors.
Photo courtesy Orsoni

Figure 65. Swiss artist Jasmin Schwitter mixes with deft mastery Vitreo (colored semitransparent glass mosaic), Brillante (transparent glass mosaic veined with enamels and avventurina stone) and dynamic inlays of Swarovski's STRASS crystal in her Topkapi collection for Trend. A medley of pinks dominates in Ambiente, a gear-toothed vertical stripe pattern from the Topkapi Collection, which includes fifteen unique patterns, each in a dominant colorway.
Photo courtesy Trend

Figure 66. Pinks, like other colors, come in a wide range of tints and tones that contrast beautifully with darker, deeper colors, in color schemes for adults. Pink and green, for example, is the quintessential Palm Beach and Hamptons color scheme. Find perfect pinks in clear, frosted and tumbled, confetti, and a host of other finishes and textures—and a range of sizes and shapes—in OriginalStyle's extensive Decorative glass tile line.
Photo courtesy OriginalStyle

Figure 67. Pink with purple undertones (remember mauve?) is an ideal accent for tiles in various shades and tints of purple. Add varying sizes and shapes for a totally captivating glass tile wall. Choose from OriginalStyle's assortment of finishes—clear, tumbled and frosted.
Photo courtesy OriginalStyle

Figure 68. Glass mosaics from Sicis adapt as readily to contemporary abstract patterns as to more familiar figurative forms of ancient glass art. Swirls in darker and lighter mosaic repeated against a gentle pink background create visual movement and depth that add a sense of three-dimensionality to wall or floor.
Photo courtesy Sicis

Figure 69. Shocking Pink (given the name by legendary fashion designer Elsa Schiaparelli) enlivens the large-scale quilt-like block pattern guaranteed to wake up any dull wall. With design confidence, opaque glass tiles from Trend's agave A Lux Collection cover the surface wallpaper-like floor-to-ceiling and wall-to-wall. A wide range of colors and matte and shining finishes make it easy to create unique colorways.
Photo courtesy Trend

Figure 70. Put a pool in the pink—literally. Sprinkling pick-me-up pink tiles among blue—a pool favorite—green, or other color ground tiles adds a lively accent top off the walls with a Boyce & Bean Pool Liner mounted on clear up/out facing tape which makes it easy for the installer to control spacing. The ½-inch thick liners refract light wonderfully.
Photo courtesy Boyce & Bean Natural Glass & Clay Co.

Figure 71. Pink glass tile adds warm dazzle to a wide border surrounding a cool-blue pool.
Photo courtesy Walker Zanger

Figure 72. For the backsplash and hood surround, glass mosaic tile in a green-with-brown-accent gradient provide color contrast and light play that add depth and expand dimension in this gloriously sunny, superbly sophisticated kitchen by Designer Alan Cohen.
Photo by Dan Forer, courtesy Cohen Geller & Associates

Figure 73. The Terrain collection by Oceanside Glasstile is a stunning group of Art Deco patterned liner bars and 3-7/8x3-7/8-inch decorative tiles. They are shown in Equator, a mossy green with iridescence.
Photo courtesy Oceanside Glasstile

Eco Green

"Going green" currently means keeping the ecosystem in mind. Many glass tile manufacturers are doing that. Some, including Bedrock and Sandhill use 100 percent recycled glass to create glass tile. Sandhill literature states that the company's 100 percent recycled-glass fused-glass technology uses one-half the energy required to produce ceramic tile, and one-fourth the energy to make cast-glass tile. Other companies use a large percentage of recycled glass in eco-conscious manufacturing processes. In October 2008, Trend introduced a collection that contains eighty percent of post-consumer recycled glass. Check on-line to find out about a specific company's "green" program.

Green is Mother Nature's color of choice for growing things. It is the color we think of when we think of Spring. Naturally, plant names describe their distinctive greens; i.e., forest, spruce, willow, moss, fern, and grass.

Fruits and vegetables lend their names. Pea green—the scrumptious slightly yellow, just a little gray green that looks as good on dining room walls as in the soup tureen on the table—is a favorite. Lettuce, lime, olive, apple, pear, celery, sage, mint, and the pale green inside honeydew melons are others.

Greens are also named for gems, including emeralds, turquoise, and jade.

There is the metallic verdigris, that wonderful color of aging copper.

Add to this treasure trove of greens the green-blues (or blue-greens) that include aqua and celedon. There are a host of tints and tones that blend green and blue so that it's impossible to say whether they are green—or blue.

The old saying, "Blue and green should never been seen (together)," is totally refuted in the new school of decorating that understands that pairing two cool colors is a cool, hip way to decorate (Figure 147).

As if all the greens mentioned were not enough, there is Paris Green (which interior designers call Poison Green, because its arsenic base proved poisonous), and Kelly Green (probably *not* named for movie legend Grace Kelly). KOG's beautiful embossed swirl pattern can be considered Kelly Green (Figure 82).

Not the complete encyclopedia of greens, this list is a glimpse of the large scope of greens that inspire decorating with glorious green glass tile.

Decorating with green glass tile

Working green into a decorating scheme is probably as easy as falling off a log, since green goes with everything. At least, the *right* green will work harmoniously! The trick is to know how to select the right green.

The color green is made by combining two primary colors—blue and yellow.

Greens that have more blue, appear cooler.

Greens that contain more yellow, appear warmer.

Since "birds of a feather" really do "flock together" in design, greens with blue tones work well with colors on the cool side of the color wheel.

Yellow-toned greens work harmoniously with colors on the warm side of the color wheel.

Yellow greens

The superbly designed Florida kitchen by Alan Cohen (Figure 72) shows how the perfect mossy green glass tile becomes a visual oasis in a gloriously sunny yellow room.

In a very different vein, Trend's Liberty collection even-handedly mixes a vibrant green, yellow, and pimento (Figure 79), for an all-over, wall cover effect.

Moss and sage greens—grayed and complex—mix handsomely with Fall's rich-harvest rusts, oranges, maroons, and browns (Figure 87; Figure 106; and Figure 168b).

Pale yellow-toned greens—willow green, for example—when used in a monotone scheme create a lighter-than-air, ethereal mood (Figure 77). Texture anchors this scheme.

Greens with yellow undertones mix beautifully with colors on the warm side of the color wheel. Green and pink (see Pink) is a tried-and-true combination in all its permutations. The watermelon, with its crisp green rind and rosy pink flesh, is Nature's guide to pairing "just the right" values of each color. Pale green and pink combinations are favorites for young girl's bedrooms. A more vibrant green and pink pair is sometimes called Palm Beach pink and green, made famous in clothing by Lilly Pulitzer. The Dunis Studio bar (Figure 75) comes close. The Victorians preferred even deeper, more saturated combinations. Red and yellow join a bright green in Old Hancock Glass Tile's wonderful Fish glass tile (Figure 152).

Figure 74. The Japanese-style cool green backsplash with unique switch plates was created by Adagio Art Glass to complement a shoji-style skylight in the ceiling and a teahouse-style gazebo outside this kitchen. Adagio specializes in unique glass tiles and custom projects.
Photo by Philip Wegner Photographer, courtesy Adagio Art Glass

Figure 75. Mardi Gras-hued fused and diachronic glass accent tiles by Dunis Studios—a leading designer of extraordinary patterned tiles—add dramatic emphasis to a bold green backsplash.
Photo courtesy Dunis Studios

Figure 76. In the Color Blox Collection, Crossville's color expert, Barbara Schirmeister, devised groupings of colors in three coordinating shades and a variety of sizes and shapes. This makes it easy for the interior designer and architect to create complex monochromatic designs that elegantly integrate awkward areas—like this backsplash and exhaust fan space—transforming them into satisfying focal points.
Photo courtesy Crossville

Blue greens

Rich, dark greens with blue undertones, like the Adagio kitchen backsplash (Figure 74), add visual weight and a sophisticated coziness. Those with tumbled, uneven edges add a rustic note to interiors like the Bedrock bathroom (Figure 81). A mixture of several different complex greens add to the mood.

Light tints of green

Split-pear green (Figure 76) is not-too-light, not-too-dark, but just right for a warm, stylish kitchen. A light, indistinct grayed-green tile paired with khaki and darker brown tiles in a sophisticated design shows off sophisticated charm in Interstyle's kitchen (Figure 80).

Pale tumbled greens—grayed to an atmospheric green and blue-green as though they had been gently faded by centuries of sun—underscore a casual look in any room (Figure 88). Those with tumbled edges that look as though the ocean had dashed them about for years and years are a natural for interiors with a by-the-seaside mood (Figure 84)

Bright Mint Green, associated with the refreshing julep, refreshes interiors, too. This clear green adds punch whether used alone or mixed with a complementary color from the opposite side of the helpful color wheel. Ann Sacks offers a bright clear green in companionable penny rounds and sticks, a mini-brick-like shape.

Figures 78a-78b. Matching colors and coordinating sizes and shapes can be an interior designer's nightmare. But, Ann Sacks makes it easy with Glace Pennies and Glace Sticks, shown here in mint green and available in other colors, each with the distinctive quartz-like iridescence.
Photo courtesy Ann Sacks

Figure 77. The liquid look of glass is underscored by watercolor-like willowy green of Raindrop Sundew glass tile by Marin Designworks. Tiles and trim in various sizes and shapes add interest without disrupting the sense of serenity introduced by the forever-Spring green.
Photo courtesy Marin Designworks

Figure 79. Mosaic tile designer Giulio Candussio created the Liberty collection comprised of transparent tiles of various sizes, shapes, and closely coordinated colors that can be combined in endless combinations. This collection celebrates in a very modern way the nature of glass tile as a highly decorative element. Here, lively green is spiced with lighter, warmer colors that enhance its coolness. *Photo courtesy Trend*

Figure 80. Greens can be sharp and sassy, bold and brassy, or as subtle and sophisticated as Interstyle's complex tints and tones in this urbane kitchen backsplash. Here, brick-shaped glass tiles set in a staggered or Flemish bond handsomely complement wood-toned cabinetry.
Photo courtesy Interstyle Ceramic & Glass Tile

Figure 81. Bedrock takes "going green" quite literally, manufacturing all the company's glass tiles from 100 percent recycled glass. No pigment is added, yet, the company is able to offer tiles in a range of green, red, and other colors. Green dominates in this tub surround and wall treatment.
Photo courtesy Bedrock Industries

Figure 82. Kokomo Opalescent Glass (KOG), the oldest manufacturer of colored art glass in the United States, made this brilliant green cast glass tile featuring a swirling pattern in a custom 16x18-inch size. In addition to custom glass, KOG makes Art Glass wall tile cut to order, and Jewel wall tile in pillow form and custom sizes.
Photo courtesy KOG Hot Glass Studio

Figure 83. In Crossville's Color Blox collection, forty-four solid colors are grouped in three coordinating shades, designed to coordinate with a selection of blends. This makes it possible for designers to create richly varied monochromatic schemes, using a variety of tiles in different sizes and shapes.
Photo courtesy Crossville

Monochromatic Green Color Schemes

When only one color makes up the color scheme, then call on line and texture to add zesty contrast.

- *Mix various sizes of tiles, like the alternating bands of small mosaic and larger 4x4-in. tiles in the Crossville bathroom (Figure 83).*
- *Contrast light and dark tiles, as shown in Trend's "wallpaper" pattern (Figure 84), which combines dark, medium, and light green tiles to create a ragged trellis or lattice pattern against a white tile background.*
- *To play up the beach-house look, with "beach-glass-look" tile, use white grout and a wide (but not too wide) grout line.*
- *Vary the texture from surface to surface, as shown in the Marin bathroom (Figure 77).*

Figure 84. Looking as though they just washed up on a frothy, foamy beach, tumbled and frosted glass tiles from OriginalStyle will give any kitchen or bathroom beach house panache. Tiles are handmade, with softened corners for the tumbled-by-Nature look.
Photo courtesy OriginalStyle

Figure 85. Green goes glam in a sophisticatedly simple bathroom decked out in mosaic glass tile by mosaic artist Mariel Hautoux of Art & Maison Miami. Large-scale tile on the floor contrasts handsomely with smaller mosaic.
Photography by Sergio Fama, courtesy Art & Maison Miami

Figure 86. Trend's new FEEL collection contains about 80 percent of post consumer recycled glass and is available in 12 colors. Here, dark, medium, and light greens mix with a lighter color to create a wallpaper-like pattern.
Photo courtesy Trend

Figure 87. A medley of soft greens in Trend's new FEEL collection contrast with light and dark rust complementary colors.
Photo courtesy Trend

Blue

Blue is the favorite color of those who love blue skies, true blue friends, blue ribbon awards, blue birds of happiness, and a host of other good things associated with blue. Fabrics are some of those very good things. Perennial favorites are toile, blue-and-white checked gingham, and broad deep blue and white awning stripes in everything—upholstery, draperies, towels, tee shirts, tablecloths, and awnings! Pottery—Delft and Chinese—is another, and so are cobalt and Bristol blue glassware.

Whether singing Blue Skies or the blues, blue is calming in all its permutations, including: denim, sky, baby, royal, navy, cobalt, turquoise, blue-ribbon, robin's egg, peacock, periwinkle (a gray-blue-lavender), ink, plumbago and phlox (purplish blues), blueberry, Mediterranean (deep blue with a hint of green to warm), midnight, Delft, azure, cerulean, sapphire, and probably many more

Tip: Blue rooms, ideally cool in summer but too cool in winter, are easily transformed into cozy havens with the addition of warm-colored accents and accessories.

Blue—cool or warm

Blue—ranging from pale pastels to dark royal blue—rules the cool side of the color wheel.

Cool colors appear to recede, and this non-aggressive quality that calms, also makes blue a great tool for creating illusions of greater space in small rooms. All blues tend to work this way, although not all blues are equally cool.

Cool blues

Blues closer to green on the color wheel are tinged with green, making them quite cool (Figure 98). Its cooling influence makes blue a natural for kitchens and rooms with southern exposures. These cool blues are excellent foils for warm woods such as pine and maple, favorites for kitchen furnishings.

Figure 88. Highly refractive hand-cut glass tiles in a subtle blend of ethereal blues frame a sleek fireplace in this contemporary living room, adding just the right note of polished sparkle.
Photo courtesy Erin Adams Design

Figure 89. GlasTile creates exquisite glass tile mosaics in a wide array of blues, ranging from an icy to rich dark blues to match any mood.
Photo courtesy GlasTile

Blue and White Bath in East Hampton

Blue, the color of the ocean, is a favorite hue for bathrooms and spas all over the world, and blue-and-white a classic color scheme that grows more popular each year.

When designer Peter Falk of Falk Gordon Interiors sought out tile for a spacious bathroom in an East Hampton home, he headed for the shop with the most exotic tiles in the area—the Alan Court Showroom in the heart of this exciting village. There, Mr. Court, whose clients include America's most rich and famous—showed him beautifully coordinated glass mosaic from Oceanside Glasstile.

Figures 90a-90b. (Above and opposite) For a house in the Hamptons, Oceanside Glasstile's Arctic Sky Blend glass mosaic creates the perfect blue-and-white combination.
Photo by Christopher Ray Photography, interior design by Peter Falk, courtesy Oceanside Glasstile

Mr. Falk chose tessera in a 1x1-inch size, in Arctic Sky Blend. The sophisticated double helix design that creates a border *cum* lavatory backsplash and an accent border for the shower combines Pearl, Bohemian, and Midori. The 4x8 tile is Casa California in Moonstone. Articulated bar liners are clear.

Walls surrounding the mostly-blue tile are a crisp white that showcases the opaque tile, creating a custom, very classic blue-and-white bath.

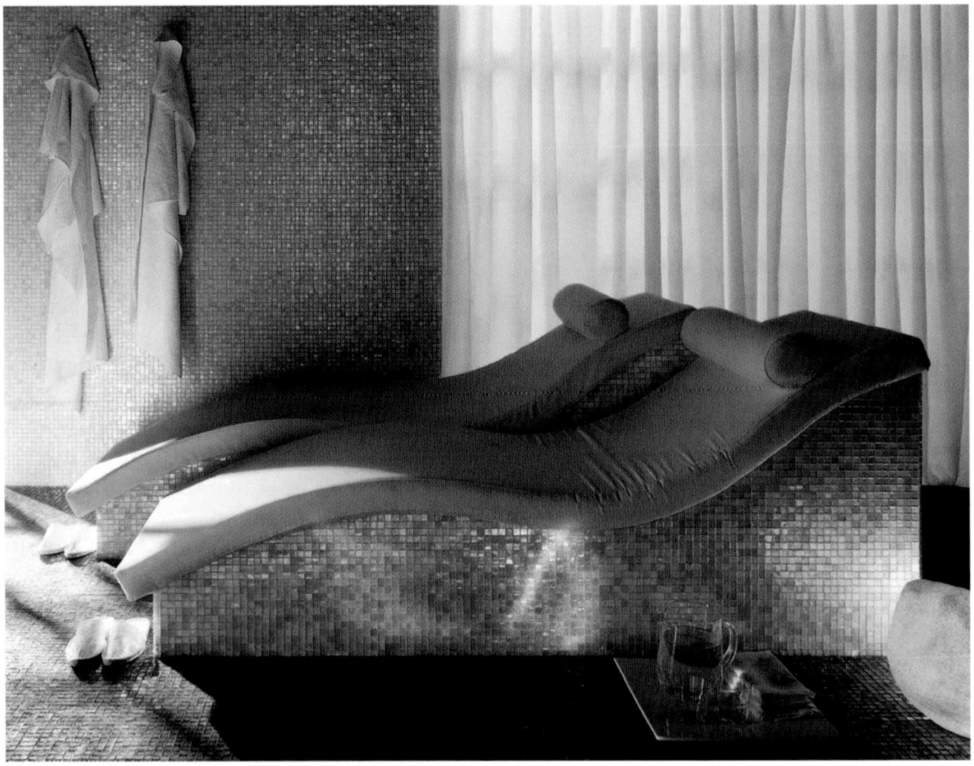

Figure 91. In a luxurious spa, custom crafted chaises wear Sicis' Glimmer mosaic glass tile, which also covers the beautifully coordinated floor and walls. A luminous iridescence lends an ethereal air to a getaway interior. *Photo courtesy Sicis*

Warm blues

Blues moving toward red on the color wheel are tinted with pink, which warms them (Figure 67). These purplish blues are harmonious companions to pinks with blue undertones.

Warmer blues create a soothing environment in Bisazza's bath with its Winterflowers wall (Figure 92), and in the spa decorated with Sicis' Glimmer glass (Figure 91). A bright and lively blue decorates the Crossville bath (Figure 99). Blue—however cool, warm, light, bright, or mysterious—gives each of these rooms a sense of serenity.

Figuring on blue

The plan for successfully designing with blue glass tile may call for a lot or a little. The decision may be entirely aesthetic, a matter of limited budget, or a combination of both. Here is how certain designers handle the question of how much, or how little tile.

One or two walls. Only a focal wall (Figure 95a), a niche (Figure 95b), or both are just what this Miami penthouse master bath needs.

A single focal point. Perhaps a small but dazzling focal point, such as a fireplace, may be all a room needs. In a contemporary living room (Figure 88), pale blue glass tiles by Erin Adams add shimmer and sheen to the fireplace even when there is no fire. Light the fire, and the tiles amplify the movement of dancing flames. Two

Figure 92. Bisazza's Winterflowers Blue, designed by Architect Carlo Dal Bianco, is a statement-making computer-generated pattern available in Vetricolor (a glass tile with smooth surface and consistent coloration) and Gloss (iridescent) tile collections. It is available in other colors, including pink and gold, and other Bisazza tile collections. *Photo by Ottavio Tomasini, styling Marcel Wanders, courtesy Bisazza*

other fireplaces (Figures 93 and 94) couldn't be more different stylistically, since one is ultra contemporary and the other sophisticatedly rustic. Yet, each is dressed in a radiant blue that enhances its role as focal point. These fireplaces attract and hold attention, so that the rest of the room plays a supporting role.

Backsplashes. Relatively small areas in kitchens and bathrooms, backsplashes are usual places for lively glass tile. In these spots, even a small amount of glass tile makes an eloquent statement. For example, two narrow rows of Lightstream glass tile add strong contrast to metal tiles, creating an emphatic border effect (Figure 96). In the Ann Sacks kitchen, Figure 97, a wall of vivid blue glass is a striking backdrop for a handsome stainless steel sink and decorative fixtures.

Blue plus

Monotone and monochromatic blue color schemes are wonderful, but do not satisfy everyone. Fortunately, blues mix and mingle beautifully with colors around the color wheel. Here are some favorite schemes.

Tricolor. The French call red, white, and blue—the tricolors—the perfect color scheme. It is the Fourth of July scheme that's perfect for backyard décor all summer long. And, depending on the values of hues, these three colors move from town to country, penthouse to cottage with equal ease.

Monet's blue and yellow scheme for Giverny inspires kitchens all over the country, including that of a neighbor's in San Antonio, Texas, who has never visited Giverny. The two kitchens by David Stimmel, principal in the Stimmel Consulting Group interpret this scheme, giving it an American accent. A living room in Figure 134a translates it, flawlessly. And a pool detail, by Mariel Hautoux (Figure 23c), re-states yellow and blue as a most happy combination. A variation, soft blue and cream, moves from the kitchen into luxurious living rooms and bedrooms.

Bright blue and bright green (Figure 147) are a smart, super cool combination of two cool colors. Once taboo—blue and green should never be seen—this combination is out and about.

Blue and pink pair in color schemes and patterns for adults (Figure 69) and children that are at home indoors and out. Pink tiles perk up blue pool surrounds (Figures 70 and 71).

- Dark blue and a lighter blue (Figure 148d) create an intriguing color scheme.

Blue and orange. Blues with a green influence contrast vividly with oranges and corals (Figure 148c).

Blues and neutrals. Blues are natural companions to beiges and grays, accentuating tranquility.

Singing the Blues

Like all colors, blues affect mood. Here are ways to let blues—and the rooms they decorate—sing.

- Use warm blues to counteract the cool light in rooms with northern exposures.
- Cool blues will tone down the warm light of southerly exposures.
- Different hues of blues work best together when they are from the same cool or warm side of the color wheel.
- Blues of contrasting values—light, medium, dark—work well together in monochromatic schemes.

Figure 93. Brilliant blue glass on a fireplace façade punctuates the space and lights up a corner with contemporary elan.
Photo courtesy Oceanside Glasstile

Figure 94. Architect David Stimmel creates a feature wall—and a unique bath—by framing lustrous glass mosaic in a strong masculine blue with rugged timbers.
Photo by Charles Meacham, courtesy Stimmel Architects

Figures 95a-95b. The South Beach (Miami) condominium of Andrea Di Giuseppe, CEO and chairman of Trend USA, is a showcase for Trend's glass tile collections. In the master bath, brilliant blue covers the shower wall and tub surround, while a lemon yellow glass tile brings sunshine, definition, and dimension to the shower stall. The floor design by LEBO/ Miami is water-jet cut agglomerate—a material made of tempered glass grit and a binding agent—that is distributed by Trend USA.

Architectural interior design, Alessandro Mendini, Atelier Mendini/Milan, photo courtesy Trend

Figure 96. Parallel rows of dazzling blue Jewel glass liners by Lightstreams contrast smartly with stainless steel tiles to animate this San Francisco Bay area backsplash. Jewel glass tile fuses complex colors with solid (not float) glass for a very durable, rich looking tile.
Photo courtesy Lightstreams

Figure 98. Adagio Art Glass matches accessories, including these cabinet knobs, to customized wall tiles for totally unique backsplashes like this one and other installations throughout the home. Custom tiles like these may fuse several layers of different glasses —iridized, amber on white, blue diachronic, mica flakes, and clear— to achieve the desired finished tile.
Photo courtesy Adagio Art Glass

Figure 97. Scintillating deep blue glass mosaic tile from Ann Sacks' Constellation Glass collection adds shimmer and sheen to a backsplash.
Photo courtesy Ann Sacks

Figure 99. Form follows function in a straightforward, uncomplicated design that shows off bold blue squares of glass tile from The Glass Blox collection by Crossville. The tiles—each a work of art—make a simple, effective backdrop for a contemporary chaise in a well-appointed bathroom.
Photo courtesy Crossville

Figure 101. Bristol blue is a sophisticated contrast to dark, mysterious BlockArt tiles from Mixed-Up-Mosaics, known for its custom designs that surprise and delight.
Photo courtesy Mixed-Up-Mosaics

Figure 100. Mosaic enriches and unites the backsplash and adjoining wall in this kitchen.
Photo courtesy Oceanside Glasstile

Custom Kitchens and Glass Tile

There are many elements which contribute to a truly custom kitchen. Designer Dave Stimmel, head of the Stimmel Consulting Group in Ambler, Pennsylvania, chose glass tile as a key style element in kitchens for two clients.

For one client, deep blue, highly iridescent tiles add sparkle and sheen, along with dramatic color.

For another, a combination of blue and yellow tiles are reminiscent of Monet's country kitchen in France. Although the Stimmel-designed kitchen is decidedly sophisticated, it too is warm and inviting.

In both kitchens, glass tile adds depth and a sense of liveliness as light and glass tile carry on a brilliant conversation.

A Tale of Two Kitchens

Figures 102a-102d. Kitchens are much lived-in areas that deserve beautifully thought out, custom designs. These two (winners of *Kitchen and Bath Business Magazine's* "Kitchen of the Year" awards) are by the Stimmel Consulting Group, headed by David Stimmel. Very different glass tiles underscore the unique look of each kitchen. *Photo courtesy Stimmel Consulting Group*

Good-Earth Colors

Good-Earth colors are . . .

The rich, ripe, mature, and complex colors of late summer gardens, including squash yellow

Fall's rich harvest of flowers, fruits, and vegetables

A wealth of spice colors in saturated golds, reds, russets, and grayed and silvered greens.

The riotous colors of turning leaves

Color names for Good-Earth colors, based largely on Nature's bounty, include: melon, mustard, ocher, saffron, cinnamon, ginger, paprika, nutmeg, kumquat, burnt orange, sage, persimmon, squash yellow, and pumpkin.

Taffy, chocolate (Figure 105), cocoa, and other earthy colors, plus the "real earth" clay colors, including terra cotta and brick, are included. So is mountain ash, named for the deep orange berries of this colorful tree. There are probably many more....

Some designers consider muted orange, terra cotta, and brown "neutrals," despite the fact that neutrals traditionally are considered the non-colors: white, black, or gray (which blends the two). Neither on the warm nor cool side of the color wheel, but existing between the two, these non-colors are neutral (see Neutrals); but, Good-Earth colors take a stand. They are decisively for room-transforming color.

Bright, young primary colors are excluded from Good-Earth tones, leaving this field to secondary or tertiary, substantial, grown-up colors. An excellent example is GlasTile's Gold Rush collection (Figure 104). Some, like Original Style's wonderful coppery brown (Figure 107), are enriched with threads of gold that add metallic gleam to their depth, sparkle, and charm.

Tiles in the Good-Earth colors are easy to live with, whether muted like those in the Original Style kitchen (Figure 106) and Sandhill's bathroom (Figure 112) or high-volume like the patchwork of harvest colors in the Walker Zanger Spaglass collection (Figure 120).

Decorating styles

These colors are at home in castle or cottage, and in Traditional and Contemporary interiors. Finish and texture of glass tile are important in determining which tile to use in which situation. Briefly,

- Castle style (Period or Modern) calls for clear, sparkling, glimmering, shimmering, iridescent and other dressy finishes and smooth, polished textures (Figure 109a).
- Cottage style is underscored by tumbled, frosted, and other rustic finishes and by equally rustic textures (Figure 112).

Figure 103. (opposite)Glass tile in rich-earth neutrals add shimmer and sheen to the complex medallion floor design in an elegant Florida dining room by Marc-Michaels.
Photo by Sargent Architectural Photography, courtesy Marc-Michaels Interior Design

Tips for Decorating With Good-Earth Colors

- Crisp pure white trim pops out against chocolate brown, creating a fresh, lively look.
- Cream-colored or ivory trims add richness and a more mature mood to a chocolate scheme.
- French and Tuscan country styles pair deep golds and paprika—an appetite stimulating combination that is great for kitchens and dining rooms.
- Sage greens and rusty reds mix as harmoniously in interiors as they do in the garden (Figure 87).

Figure 104. GlasTile's Gold Rush Collection features half-inch thick glass field tiles in popular sizes and such earthy colors as Black Hills, Dusk, Sierra, and Sierra Special. Black Gold and Sierra Gold, which come in 2x2-in. and 2x8-in. sizes, have visible gold-covered *nuggets* fired onto a black or bronze base glass, giving these tiles a unique textural look.
Photo courtesy GlasTile

Figure 105. Among Crossville's Color Blox collection of forty-four mouthwatering colors are an array of sensual neutrals that work alone, with two other coordinating shades, or in various color-hue combinations. Additionally, Crossville's color maestro, Barbara Schirmeister, has a Color Blox glass tile palette that is designed to complement other Crossville collections in other materials, including Porcelain Stone.
Photo courtesy Crossville

Figure 106. A mosaic blend of harvest colors in a tumbled, beach-washed finish provide comfort-food sensibility for kitchen design with relaxed elegance in mind. OriginalStyle has many more color combinations and finishes on its menu.
Photo courtesy OriginalStyle

Figure 107. OriginalStyle's metallic mosaics add exciting gold flecks to fabulous rich-earth colors in sparkling clear glass. The result is a scintillating surface.
Photo courtesy OriginalStyle

Figure 108. A bold abstract leaf-form executed in mosaic glass tile in positive and negative versions of rich-harvest colors is arresting wall art in a contemporary living space. A wide range of colors available in Sicis' several glass tile collections encourages such creativity.
Photo courtesy Sicis

Figures 109a-109b. Lake Garda, Ann Sacks' most successful glass field tile covers the base of the bar that separates—without closing it off—and unites the living area and kitchen in this contemporary home. Available as wall and floor tile, Lake Garda's extensive color palette of forty colors encourages blending mix-mastery. Sizes ranging from 2x2-inch decorative inserts and 2x12-inch liners (trim), to standard square (up to 8x8-in.) and brick shapes (up to 6x12-in.) encourage design creativity. Lake Garda Flooring tiles are available in a range of sizes up to 12x12-inch square.
Photo courtesy Ann Sacks

Figures 110a-110b. Walker Zanger's Spa Glass tiles in a quilt-block mix of rich harvest colors—choose from twenty colors in the collection—add great zest to walls and island front in a bright kitchen.
Photo courtesy Walker Zanger

Figures 111a-111c. Glass tile inserts in a seating area fireplace surround coordinate with similar inserts in the adjoining kitchen backsplash, unifying the two areas and adding beauty spots to each.
Photo courtesy KOG Hot Glass Studio

Figure 112. Sandhill's soft and gentle palette of thirty-size sumptuous colors is easy on the earth's ecosystem, since the tile is made from 100 percent recycled glass.
Photo courtesy Sandhill Industries

Figure 113. The Liberty collection by mosaic tile designer Giulio Candussio offers the architect and interior designer transparent, hand-cut tiles of various sizes, shapes, and closely coordinating and decidedly contrasting colors that can be combined in endless ways for custom decorative effects. Here, a rich, sunny yellow gains greater dimension by being paired with contrasting colors.
Photo courtesy Trend

Neutrals

Strictly speaking, true or pure neutrals are *non-colors*—white or black—but, for practical purposes, we call them colors. (Figure 129)

Because these neutrals are *not* colors, they are neither warm nor cool, neither advance nor recede. They stand in *neutral territory* between the warm and cool sides of the color wheel. Ergo, they are neutrals. That is the theory.

Practice often elbows theory aside, however, so the neutral palette is expanded to include beiges and grays.

Further, in the "give an inch and they will take a mile" spirit, some designers call any color that is not aggressive and makes a great background a neutral—including navy blue, dark browns, and very dark greens. Others, taking greater liberty, call red, pink, orange, and almost any color that makes a great-looking background a neutral. Which is like saying that pink is the navy blue of India, or brown is the new black, and so on. But, keeping the neutral record straight, neutrals are white, black, beige, and grays (including greige, which blends beige and gray, and taupe, which is a grayed tan with a little brown so that some call it "mouse.").

Neutrals' Temperatures

While technically speaking, neutrals are neither cool nor warm, real-life neutrals really are. It is important to note this when using any neutral with one or more colors, since cools relate to cools, and warms harmonize with warm colors.

Cool Neutrals

Black and white, the strongest of all neutral design statements, are super cools. This classic combination works in any and all decorating styles and periods. The finish and texture of glass tile will indicate whether the tile is best suited for a formal or informal room. Certain textures, like that of Innovative Glass Elements' white tile (Figure 125), is adaptable and appropriate for many different interiors.

Call the successful pairing of black and white a "harmony of opposites," but black and white are always in dynamic tension, in a power struggle between two equals. Used in equal portions, a stalemate results in stability (very useful in rooms made chaotic with numerous openings and other busy architectural elements).

Use more white, and black becomes a powerful accent (Figure 125). One small black dot or bar will stand out emphatically in a field of white. A grid pattern in black against a white background (Figure 120) will capture and hold attention.

Use more black, creating a sense of drama and mystery, and white will serve as punctuation (Figure 124). Black, as sole color, stands alone beautifully, but add a single subtle other color, like that in Crossville's backsplash (Figure 123), and a chiascuro (light and shadow) effect adds even greater depth and fascination.

Designer Rudy Santos included modular black and white tiles in his *Fantastiques*™ collection that make it easy for any designer to create custom combinations in these two colors. In Chapter Five, Sizes and Shapes, we show the Concept Boards from the *Fantastiques*™ *Black-and-White* group that show the endless possibilities—all striking.

White as a room's sole color has been extremely popular in recent years. It is a great unifying element for rooms with a lot of line content (doors, windows, and so on) and a foolproof scheme for houses with open floor plans. An iridescent finish for Bisazza's Righe Bianco white-pearl tiles adds unexpected flashes of color that relieve the starkness of an all-white interior (Figure 121).

Gray, the signature color of the late, very talented designer, Angelo Donghia, who made gray chic, can be either warm or cool. Names often provide clues as to whether the gray is warm or cool. For example, cool grays based on metals include pewter, gunmetal, and steel. Dove sounds gentle, but dove gray is cool. Ash, oyster, charcoal, and mouse describe warmer grays. Look for all those in glass tile.

The warm gray tile in the Ann Sacks bathroom (Figure 117) is as atmospheric as drifting fog with sunshine breaking through. Warm matte grays in Walker Zanger's Vintage collection inspired by onyx, are less chilling and richer than pure white for an all-white bathroom.

Gray blends with other neutrals for most interesting effects. Interstyle's black-white-and-gray blend (Figure 126) with its blue undertones is super cool and very chic. Walker Zanger's Mondrian tile mixes black, white, and a wonderful warm blued gray.

Warm neutrals

At one point, the term "earth tones" was used to describe a palette of light, earthy colors such as desert sand, beige, and taupe. These un-demanding, peaceful neutrals comprise a favorite palette, and not just in the American Southwest, which inspired them. In matte finishes and rustic textures, they emphasize informality. In fine finishes and textures, these colors create a mood of great luxury and urbane sensitivity.

A case in point: The smartly designed Oceanside Glass Tile bathroom (Figures 119a and 119b) makes the most of space by placing a long, narrow shower niche along one wall, leaving space for passage. Glass walls keep the space looking open and airy. They also show off a blend of beautiful taupe colored glass tile. The same tile creates wrap-around tub and lavatory backsplashes, for great design continuity.

Figure 114. Wall areas clad in Architectural Ceramics' Seta glass tile seem to float away, creating a warm but airy look.

Figure 115. The plane's the thing in this room of multi-levels, each contributing to an out-of-the-box, transporting mood.

Easy-to-live-with neutrals become dynamic in the hands of sophisticated architects and designers like Jordan Goldstein and Jill Goetsel. This space, created for the Washington Design Center in the nation's Capitol, shows how.

Gensler's Neutral Media Room

By design, this new age family room is a warm, inviting media room—a space that welcomes the entire family.

Designers Jordan Goldstein, AIA, and Jill Goebel, IIDA of Gensler, the country's leading architectural firm, took their cue from a traditional Japanese home. The room offers an elevated plane for re-orienting oneself within the space and a sunken lounge area that is a tranquil nest.

The experience of moving through the space is enhanced by being able to move from one level to the other. Animated, light-refracting glass tile adds another dimension to the sense of movement.

The tranquil color scheme—a key to the room's restful mood—begins with a light, warm neutral color discreetly accented by a gently contrasting color.

Blending beautifully with the wall color, but remaining a distinct accent and asset, is Seta glass tile in a gloss finish from Architectural Ceramics. The 3x6-inch tile is oriented in a restful horizontal position. The tile is set in a simple stacked or subway style. With no grout joints, tiles butt together, creating a better interplay of light and display of tile color. This helps the beauty of the glass tiles to read more clearly on all planes.

—based on comments by Mr. Goldstein and Ms. Goebel

Figure 116. (opposite) The wet bar is a decorative oasis set in a depth-expanding niche. *Architecture and Interior Design, Jordan Goldstein, AIA, and Jill Goetsel, IIDA, Gensler; Photos courtesy Washington Design Center, Washington, DC*

Figure 117. Northwest Glass tiles from Ann Sacks define the lavatory niche and add refreshing contrast in this stylish bathroom design. Coordinating tiles clad the tub surround base.
Photo courtesy Ann Sacks

Figure 118. Walker Zanger's Vintage collection is crafted by pouring together transparent and opaque glass to produce a marbleized surface. A sense of pattern and movement enlivens and enriches. There are fourteen colors in the collection—including onyx in a matte finish as shown.
Photo courtesy Walker Zanger

Figures 119a-119b. The Hamilton's smartly designed bathroom tile reads as greige, adding cool sophistication and the right degree of warmth to this inviting space. *Photo courtesy Oceanside Glastile*

Figure 120. Divide and conquer a dull wall with a sophisticated grid, a smart alternative to traditional panels. Worked out in chic white, black, and clear tiles from Crossville's Color Blox collection, the grid-dressed wall becomes focal point and star—a work of art that eliminates the over-the-sofa painting.
Photo courtesy Crossville

Figure 121. Bisazza's Righe glass tile by architect Carlo Dal Bianco has the look of elegant wallpaper. The Righe pattern—inspired by classical textiles—comes in three colors, including Righe Bianco (white, shown), Righe Blu (light blue), and Righe Rosa (pink). Righe is available in two finishes: Vetricolor, a uniformly square tile with cushioned and beveled edges, a smooth surface, and consistent color that is impervious to UV rays and fade resistant and Gloss, which has an iridescent effect.
Photo by Federico Cedrone, styling Beatrice Rossetti, credit Il Centrotavola, Venini, courtesy Bisazza

Figure 122.(opposite) Walker Zanger's Mondrian translucent glass tiles are inspired by twentieth century abstract painter Piet Mondrian. The nine patterns in the collection—like Mondrian's paintings—emphasize crisp lines and strong, boldly contrasting colors, including black and white.
Photo courtesy Walker Zanger

Figure 123. Certain dark glass tiles are complex colors containing a lot of black so that they have the same powerful impact plus added warmth. Crossville's Glass Blox collection contains a number of such colors. Here, a mini-brick tile in a staggered or Flemish bond works effectively as black with magical refractive and reflective properties that make it a continually changing canvas as light, like an artists' brush, moves across it.
Photo courtesy Crossville

Figure 124. Vidrotil's dramatic Color 340 glass tile, reading as a dark neutral, lights up this dramatic bathroom by Architect Belkis Dutra for 2004 Casa Cor, Brazil's most renowned show house.
Photography by Sagrilo, architecture/interior design by Belkis Dutra, courtesy Vidrotil

Figure 125. Strong-impact black and white glass tiles gain new dimension when pattern and texture are added. Innovative Glass Elements' Anthology Patterns of glossy-surfaced tiles with soft corners—available in a range of motifs and textures—are translucent.
Photo courtesy Innovative Glass Elements

Figure 126. Blending muted grays and gray-greens with black warms up a cool color scheme and adds interest.
Photo courtesy Interstyle

Figure 127. Can there be a more sophisticated color scheme than black and white, or its softer version, gray-and-white? Pair these non-colors, and perhaps muted colors in a restrained palette for chiascuro effect, for an elegant, timeless look. This interior by Brazilian architects Claudia Lorensini and Murillo Vaccari used Vidrotil's Rhythms Collection mosaics in four colors to achieve the beautifully patterned walls in this elegant interior. *Photography by Marco Pinto, courtesy of the architects and Vidrotil*

Figure 128. When Brazilian architect Rogerio Cordeiro looked for glass tiles with which to execute his vision, he chose a variety of tiles from several Vidrotil groups, including three sizes of mosaics from the Borders Collection, floor and wall mosaics, and ¾-inch mosaics for the countertop—and in Color 610! And the vision is spectacular.
Photography by Marco Pinto, architecture Rogerio Cordeiro, courtesy Vidrotil

Figure 129. Limiting a palette to black and white need not confine. A concept board from Rosan Imports' *Fantastiques* collection by Rudy Santos expands design possibilities. For many, many more possibilities see five concept boards from this group in Chapter 5, Sizes and Shapes.
Photo courtesy Rosan Imports

Color and Pattern Power

Figure 130. Red and white glass tiles by Trend star in a sassy dressing room.
Photo courtesy Trend

An almost identical trellis pattern in the two same-size rooms shown here creates a sense of movement that makes each room seem spacious and gracious. Yet, because color is a powerful and distinctive mood-maker, these rooms are very different places.

Colors on the warm side of the color wheel attract, advance, cause a rise in respiration and heartbeat rates, and generally generate a great deal of heat and excitement. Unify Trend's red glass mosaic walls with red countertop and floor and *viola*—the room is one joyous shout out.

Cool colors appear to recede, leaving the viewer a sense of ample space in which to luxuriate. For the green bathroom, Architect Warren Bohn and Interior Designer Kelly Woodruff chose a gentle willow green to create a cool, calm, and collected mood of well-being. Large format floor tiles echo the scale of the trellis pattern on the glass tile wall and dark wood add a warm, grounding note. Clearly, this is a space for one who has no desire to shout and can well afford to speak in a whisper.

Alone, each is strong. Together, color and pattern are a dynamic duo

Figures 131. Pale green glass tile creates a home-as-haven mood.
Photo courtesy Warren Bohn, AIA

Chapter Three
Pattern

Blank walls cry out for pattern—that wonderful combination of line and color that provides focus for the eye, food for thought, and warmth for the heart. When Italian designer Francesco Lucchese of Studio Lucchese Design was asked to transform the old glass and aluminum Alexander Building in Sofia, Bulgaria, into a truly hospitable hotel, he chose to add warmth with glass tile in floral motifs. The exterior lobby (with its grand staircase), and each guest room, features a different floral pattern. The successful transformation prompted the name—Hotel Les Fleurs (Figures 132a-132d). Powerful pattern, able to transform impersonal commercial space, is even more welcome in residences, where personal style is so important.

Lucchese's use of glass tile on the façade of a building, as well as the interior, underscore the point that every space is improved by pattern, however bold or subtle. A space with no pattern is poor indeed. Glass tile provides a wealth of pattern possibilities, including ready-made patterned tile as well as a rainbow of colored tiles in a dizzying array of sizes and shapes for custom designs.

Figures 132a-132d. (Above, opposite, and next page) Studio Lucchese Design added warmth and distinction to the exterior and interior of the Hotel Les Fleurs, Sofia, Bulgaria, with outsized floral patterns executed in mosaic glass tile by Trend.
Photo by Arnaldo dal Bosco, courtesy Trend

Ready-made Patterns

Ready-made patterned or decorative tiles are available in one or more of three formats—individual or sheet-mounted mosaics, single standard-size tiles, and panels.

Single (individual) decorative tiles

Noteworthy among decorative standard-size tiles are those in this chapter, including figurative, abstract, geometric, and ethnic patterns. There are also florals, stylized florals, and patterns based on fabrics. Fashionable animal prints are realized in glass tile, and so are fossil-like motifs and nature-inspired shells. Dunis Studios has a host of extraordinary tiles in romantic geometric designs (Figures 148a-148d).

Mixed-Up-Mosaics patterned tiles include a fabric-inspired plaid (Figure 156a) and op-art elliptical circles (Figures 156b-156d), as well as tiger and giraffe patterns (Figures 157a-157b) that are décor classics.

UltraGlas Tile's Moorish-look tile, Figure 140 references Mediterranean architecture, while Trikeenan's patterned Glass Windows collection is inspired by Gothic stained glass windows. This collection is extensive, and intricately patterned tiles (Figure 148e) may be installed in any number of ways to unique effect.

Be Aware, and Be Happy!

Patterned tiles (see the Dunis and Trikeenan—and UltraGlas's Diagonal Radius tiles, Figure 150) often may be installed in any one of several possible configurations, but beware. When patterned tiles—especially directional patterns—are used as field (background) tiles, the result will be the introduction of yet another pattern. There will be a pattern-on-pattern effect. A good example is Trikeenan's Sanctuary tile (Figure 148e) from the Glass Window's collection. This tile, when installed, results in both an undulating vertical and a diagonal stripe—in addition to the surface pattern and the grid-like pattern of grout lines. This adds up to four patterns—what a boon to the lover of the pattern-on-pattern look!

End pattern results are not always easy to envision. Prevent unwelcome surprises by considering the possibilities, perhaps with a "dry run" layout before installing the tiles.

The host of other patterned tiles in this chapter and throughout the book include geometric and figurative designs on a flat plane (Marin Designwork's Wave, Figure 137b) or in bas relief (Shells by UltraGlass, Figure 154).

Tiles in one pattern may be used alone as a ground tile, or may be mixed with solid-color tiles. They may also be used merely as accents. See Dunis patterned tiles incorporated into a border/backsplash in a bathroom (Figure 75).

Ready-made large-scale patterns

Some manufacturers offer ready-made large-scale, even whole-wall patterns composed of individual mosaic tiles. Several can be seen in this chapter and throughout the book.

Bisazza's super-sized Winterflowers pattern (Figure 133b), for example, is a computer-generated pattern based on old textured French fabrics, and realized in three complementary tile collections. These include Bisazza glass, Vericolor (a square tile with cushioned and beveled edges, and Oro BIS, which has 24-karat gold leaf sandwiched between two layers of glass. This variety of finishes among these three collections create depth due to varying intensities of refraction and reflection, and add texture to the pattern. Bisazza tiles are mounted.

Trend's Magic Way (Figure 138) and Coral Ambiente (Figure 143) are other examples of beautifully thought out whole-wall designs. Some are available in various colorways.

Some manufacturers of gradients or blends of small mosaic tiles offer pre-selected combinations and deliver them in large panels.

Figures 133a-133b. Bisazza's Winterflower pattern is big, bold, and beautiful. The stylized pattern, a contemporary riff on ancient and formal textile patterns, is at home anywhere. It is available in three different Bisazza tile collections, including Vetricolor, Le Gemme (avventurina stone adds shimmer to the mix), and Oro Bis (its glow comes from 24-karat gold leaf between layers of glass). *Photos courtesy Bisazza*

Figures 134a-134b. Bright solid contemporary colors in Crossville's Glass Blox collection provide the palette for a large-scale "wallpaper" pattern with a repeated stylized floral motif. Such a design is effective for a focal wall or niche. *Photo courtesy Crossville*

Creating a Pattern of One's Own

Creating a **pattern** of one's own can be challenging. But the fun begins with working with **line** (planning layouts by size and shape), then adding **color.**

Drawing the Line

To decide what size and shape to use, consider whether you will use tiles in small, medium, or large-format sizes and in which shapes.

Three bathrooms in this chapter (Figures 142, 144, and 155) are great examples of successful, individualistic approaches. Since all are in a blue palette, it is easy to focus on the sizes and shapes of tile used to create pattern and the contribution they make to the success of each design.

Ann Sacks' Lake Garda bathroom (Figure 142) uses pattern to call attention to two key areas, the raised tub and the shower niche. The clean-cut design of the space calls for emphatic but non-fussy tiles. A medley of blue and white slender medium-sized rectangular tiles installed vertically and staggering the colors creates an interesting stylized flame-stitch pattern that is just right for an easy-elegance mood.

The Hakatai bathroom (Figure 144) uses a delightful blend of blue and white mosaic to "wallpaper" all walls in a random pattern that keeps the eye flitting, underscoring the room's fresh, youthful mood. Weighting white tiles at the bottom and top create "borders" that finish the design. The effect is beautiful and unique.

The Oceanside Glass Tile bathroom (Figure 155) creates a sense of space-expanding unity with a monochromatic blue color scheme in small-scale mosaic tile. Two design elements move the eye, relieving any feeling of cramped or confined space. These include tile laid in a dynamic diagonal on the floor to defy the "box" shape of the bathroom, and an emphatic Greek wave border that moves the eye upward and around the walls.

Working with small-scale mosaics

Mosaic tile, an ancient size and shape, is an enormously flexible design tool for creating either small- or large-scale pattern. Usually, mosaics are 1x1-inch squares (mounted in sheets as large as 11-3/4 x 11-3/4-inch sizes), or smaller (like Dolce's "chicklet," Figure 208), which are also mounted for installation ease. Some companies mount a custom mosaic blend on panels as large as 8-foot long.

The Hakatai and Oceanside bathrooms use mosaics to create small-scale patterns; but compare these with the strikingly different, large-scale Trend Coral Ambiente irregular stripe (Figure 143) and the intricate Magic Way block patterns (Figure 139). These over-sized patterns are so strong that a second look is needed to realize that the pattern magic is not done with mirrors, but with mosaics.

If ready-made patterns-to-go are not the answer but do inspire, visit a tile showroom that makes designing with mosaic easy by providing tessarae and templates for experimenting with various combinations. At the launching of Trend USA's Miami showroom, these tools, openly available to the interior designers present, were a big hit!

Some companies provide design-on-line programs. This is especially true of companies such as Hakatai, which sell gradients or blends of mosaic tiles like those in the Hakatai bath (Figure 144) and the Marc-Michaels kitchen (Figure 4). The gradient tiles contribute to the complexity of the design in the Marc-Michaels kitchen, adapt to the Moorish-influenced architectural shaped hood, and elegantly underscore the unique mood of this kitchen that deftly weds Moorish and Modern.

A complicated design like that in the Marc-Michaels kitchen inspires, but can also seem daunting. Exploring your design concepts, and the blends needed to realize them on-line, should put fear to rest.

Focusing on Design

Before starting your tile design, do as professionals do; that is, decide key issues that will speed the right size, shape, texture, and color tile selection. And, it will be easier to resist a tempting tile that would derail the design.

- ***Mood:*** *Formal, casual, casual elegance, sophisticated, rustic, quaint, or other?*
- ***Style:*** *Historic, traditional, contemporary, eclectic, personal?*
- ***Area to cover:*** *One or more walls, floor, ceiling or some combination?*
- ***Scale:*** *Small, moderate, or larger-than-life?*

Figure 135. A freewheeling running ribbon pattern in mosaic tessera from Vitralia, Megaron's glass tile collection, has a casual quality that seems especially contemporary.
Photo courtesy Megaron Italian Design & Mosaics

Figure 136. A ribbon-like running vine and flower pattern is an ancient concept made current by mosaic artists Allison Goldenstein and Leslie Provazano, owners of Mixed-Up-Mosaics. Here, the firebox surround with its new/old vine/flower motif adds fresh fire to a period French mantel.
Photo courtesy Mixed-Up-Mosaics

Figures 137a-137b. Marin Designworks offers ribbon patterns in several forms, including the liner-bar-thin cut-glass ribbon that can be cut to various widths and inserted into a background of field or border tile. It can be repeated in a ribbon-pattern Oceana Wave tile. *Photos courtesy Marin Designworks*

Figure 138. (opposite) Tile used in large-scale patterns, floor-to-ceiling and wall-to-wall as one would hang wallpaper, is not for the faint of heart—nor is it for the fickle decorator who thrives on change. Trend's Magic Way geometric, quilt-like pattern makes a strong and lasting taste-setting statement that is at the same time ancient, modern, and ultimately timeless. *Photo courtesy Trend*

Working with standard, medium-scale tiles

Generally, common tiles sizes include 4x4, 4x6, 4x8, 5x5, 6x6, 8x8, 6x12, and 12x12 inches. All are scaled to work well in most interiors. They also allow for a big variety of installation patterns. The most familiar are:

- Straight bond or grid pattern. Tiles are laid in rows for very stable effect.
- Running bond. Tows are staggered, eliminating a straight grout line.
- Diamond. Square tiles laid on-point to look like a diamond and create a dynamic diagonal.
- Herringbone. Tiles laid in alternate horizontal/vertical arrangements create a zigzag pattern. Rows of alternating colors add excitement.
- Basket weave. Tiles appear to interleaf in a woven pattern that creates a more open, less confining look.
- Parquet. Tiles are laid in opposite directions, like wood flooring squares.
- Corridor. Horizontal and vertical rows are alternated, and seem directional and traffic moving.

There are myriad ways to vary basic layout patterns, including:

- inserting small diamond-shaped decorative tiles, the core of four square tiles
- enlarge a grid pattern by interspersing decorative border tiles between tiles laid in a grid
- create a pinwheel by combining different sized square- and rectangular-shaped tiles
- creating an "area" rug (square or round) by using border tile to mark "rug" edges, then laying tile on the diagonal, or creating a pattern within the borders to heighten the "rug" effect.

Up the pattern ante by mixing and matching modular tiles or using three or more tile sizes to create complex patterns such as hopscotch, steppingstone, windmill, multi-pinwheel, cartwheel, lattice, trellis, clustered trellis, modular diagonal, and more!

Pile on the pattern by adding one or more borders—simple or complex. The idea with borders is to add one where the eye expects to see it. That is usually at chair rail or ceiling height. A high-ceilinged bathroom might actually look wonderful with three borders: one at chair rail height, a broad border at a standard 8- or 12-foot height, and a narrower border nearer the ceiling.

Large-format tiles and pattern

Generally, creating pattern involving large-format tiles is much like working with medium-sized tiles. All the layout methods that result in pattern can be applied to large-format tiles. What becomes important in choosing to work with large-format tiles is to scale them to the space. And keep in mind that some of the layouts are identified with particular historic styles and patterns. The contemporary rooms tend to lay these tiles with narrow or no grout lines and little or no pattern.

Most frequently, large-format tiles are used as flooring and in bathrooms as tub surrounds. Less often, they are used on interior walls.

Adding Color

Color and line are equal partners in most patterns. And when color is added to a simple, straightforward grid pattern (like alternating red and black squares in Figure 55, or small decorative dots, Figure 54) the pattern takes on a very different, far more vibrant look.

Color is so energetic, that mixing several strong colors in a design makes it seem to leap off the wall. The stronger the colors, the greater the wow power. Great examples are the kitchen (Figures 110a-110b), and Mixed-Up-Mosaics' Funky Block bar (Figure 57). Of course, the quieter the colors, the more serene the space.

Mixing colors with various shaped and sized tiles results in murals (Figure 139), medallions (Figures 111a-111c), "area rugs" (Figure 160), and other vital focal points.

Many of the interiors in this book mix two or more colors and should prove good guides to creating a pattern. For more about color and how to design with it, see Chapter 2, with its many color palettes.

Glass Tile Pattern Versus Wallpaper

Several reasons why glass tile might be a better choice than wallpaper (or wall covering) for adding pattern to walls, floors, and ceilings are that glass tile:

- *Does not fade (look for cast (color added during manufacturing) or fused glass)*
- *Does not stain*
- *Edges do not fray*
- *Wipes clean*
- *Is three-dimensional (because of light refraction), adding visual depth to the surface*
- *Is animated—refracting, reflecting, sparking, shimmering—interacting with light in a perpetual, lively dance*
- *Has a long lifespan*

Figure 139. Mosaic artist Julie Richey's Umbrian Villa mural is a 10-in. x 8-ft. backsplash with a view. The landscape pierces this usually dark, flat space, offering the viewer a vast horizon that frees from confining space. Refracted light from the glass tiles animates the scene.
Photo by Stacy Dail Bratton Photography, courtesy Julie Richey Mosaics

Figure 140. An intricate pattern reminiscent of ancient Moorish patterns is ready-to-install, eliminating what would otherwise be a time-consuming job.
Photo courtesy UltraGlas Tile

Figure 141. As if the more than fifteen patterns in fifteen glass colors were not enough, design wizards combine any one of the patterns in Trikeenan's Glass Windows Collection in various ways.
Photo courtesy Trikeenan Tileworks

Figure 142. Perspective alters pattern perception, as seen in this bathroom, where tiles from the Ann Sacks Lake Garda Collection take on a distinct flame-stitch appearance in the shower stall that is not as readily noticed in the tub surround base.
Photo courtesy Ann Sacks

Figure 143. Small pieces of glass tile tessera in a wide range of colors can be used as gradients. They lend themselves readily to complex geometric designs that are simultaneously profound and subtle patterns. Boldness of line depends on the degree of contrast between light and dark, warm and cool colors—all easily controlled by the designer. Ambiente –a ragged stripe design shown here is from the Topkapi Collection of Vitreo and Brillante glass tiles enhanced with three-dimensional Swarkovski STRASS crystal tile inlays by Swiss artist Jasmine Schwitter for Trend.
Photo courtesy Trend

Figure 144. Gradients or blends that randomly mix a variety of colored mosaic tessera take on a greater or lesser sense of pattern, depending on distribution of colors. Here, clustering white tiles near the bottom of the wall and scattering them loosely up the wall creates an abstract flowering pattern or movement in the remodeled Malden home bathroom.
Photo courtesy Hakatai Enterprises

Figure 145. Architect Selma de Sa Moreira wittily combines several different colors of glorious glass tile from Vidrotil in a complex design involving multi-borders and patterns in subtle movements. This fascinating design—full of translucence and shimmer—is complex without seeming busy—a sure sign of genius at work.
Photography by Victor Fernandes, design by Architect Selma de Sa Moreira, courtesy Vidrotil

Figure 146. A very stylish mermaid with a gold-touched tiara lounges in an enchanted pool—made enchanting with mosaic glass tile designs by mosaic artist Mariel Hartoux, head of Miami-based Art & Maison.
Photo by Sergio Fama, courtesy Art & Maison Miami

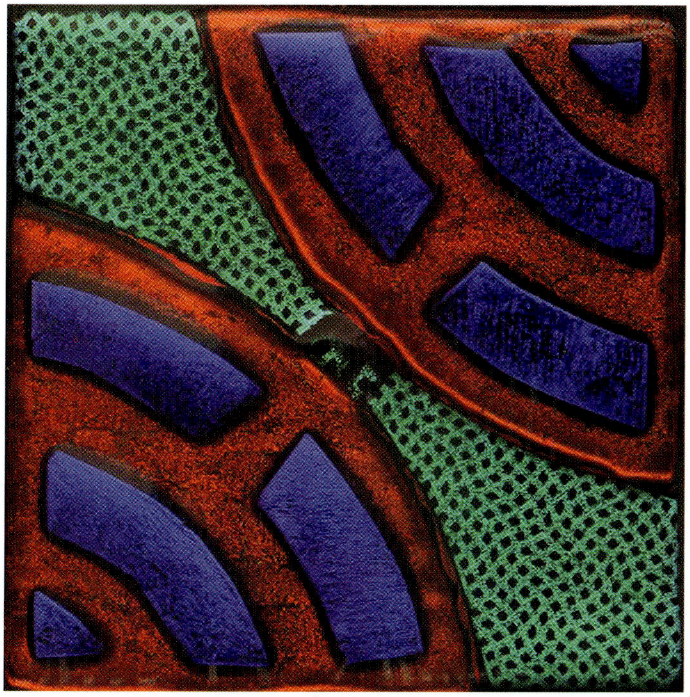

Figures 148a-148d. Dunis Studio creates wonderfully patterned tiles that can effectively be used as decorative accents for plain background tiles. When using these tiles as a background, experiment with layouts that permit viewing before installation, since combining these patterned tiles will probably create yet another pattern. *Photo courtesy Dunis Studio*

Figure 147. (opposite) An imaginative designer often needs very little with which to create exciting pattern. Here, rows of different color, same-size tessera set on-point (diamond-like) result in a dynamic zigzag stripe. The greater the contrast, the stronger the pattern in mosaic glass tiles from Trend. *Photo courtesy Trend*

Figure 148e. Trikeenan's Windows collection features patterns based on antique stained glass window motifs. When installed, these multi-patterned tiles create still other patterns.
Photo courtesy Trikeenan

Figure 149. Mosaic designer Erin Adams' Quilts Collection features hand-assembled layers of colored glass that are kiln-fired to fuse them into American-quilt-like patterns. Tiles are mesh-mounted in 12x12-inch open seam segments. They are available in a variety of colorways and in three sizes (1.5x1.5 inch, 2.5x2.5 inch, and a 2.5x3 inch brick shape.
Photo courtesy Erin Adams

Figure 150. The "Diagonal Radius Design" by UltraGlas is an asymmetrical pattern that can be installed in any number of directions to create a variety of provocative patterns. The hand-made glass tile, shown in Peach, is available in thirty-one standard luminous colors. Custom colors may be specified.
Photo courtesy UltraGlas

Figure 151. Cartebo adds a fossil-like pattern to a tile that can be used en masse or as a decorative element with other plain glass, ceramic, stone, or metal tiles to stunning effect.
Photo courtesy Cartebo

Figure 152. Old Hancock Glass Tile, under principal designer Chris Baker-Salmon, has patented a process that features bas-relief imagery that is decorated with fired-on (fused) glass color and is visible through the body of clear glass tile, which has a smooth face. Here, a stylish fish design in a variety of glorious glass colors is highly decorative and decidedly thematic. Custom designs may be specified.
Photo courtesy Old Hancock Glass Tile

Figure 153. Oceanside Glasstile's Super Lattice from the Facets Collection, is a delightful pattern woven in Incense and Cane colors. A trellis pattern makes a wall look two-dimensional so that a room seems more spacious. There are six borders in this collection and three different field tiles.
Photo courtesy Oceanside Glasstile

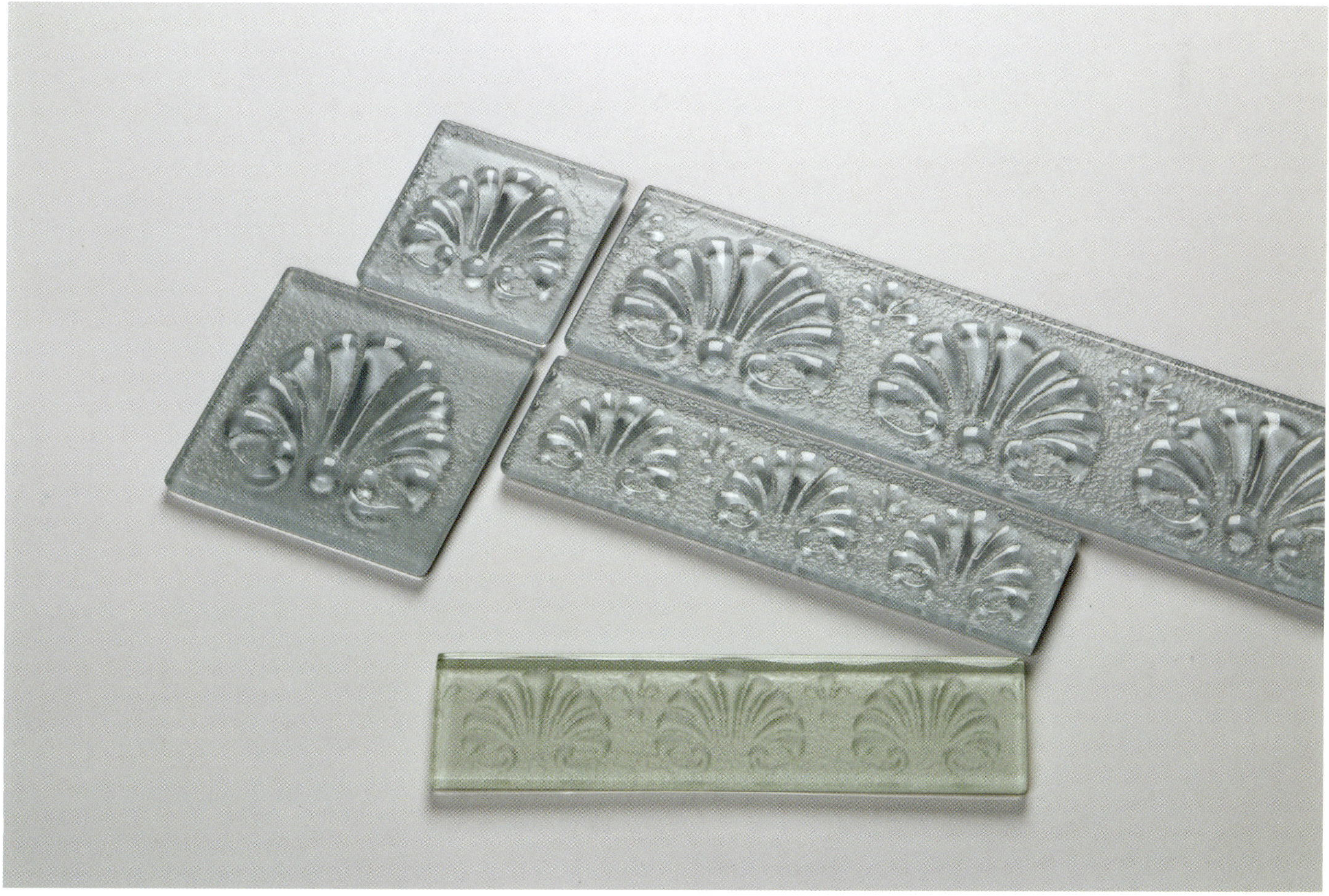

Figure 154. Designs with patterns such as Shells from the Neo collection by UltraGlas underscore interior design themes. A variety of sizes and shapes make it easy to create an entire wall of Shells or use this patterned tile as a decorative accent. UltraGlas tiles are available in thirty-one standard colors.
Photo courtesy UltraGlas

Figures 156a-156c. Mixed-Up-Mosaic creates a medley of updated style-asserting patterns—plaid, elliptical circles, and parquet—that demonstrate the tremendous design flexibility of glass tile.
Photo courtesy Mixed-Up-Mosaics

Figure 155. (opposite) Mosaic in contrasting colors create a strong figurative border with an ancient wave motif. On the floor, mosaic laid on the diagonal creates a diamond-patterned floor.
Photo courtesy Oceanside Glasstile

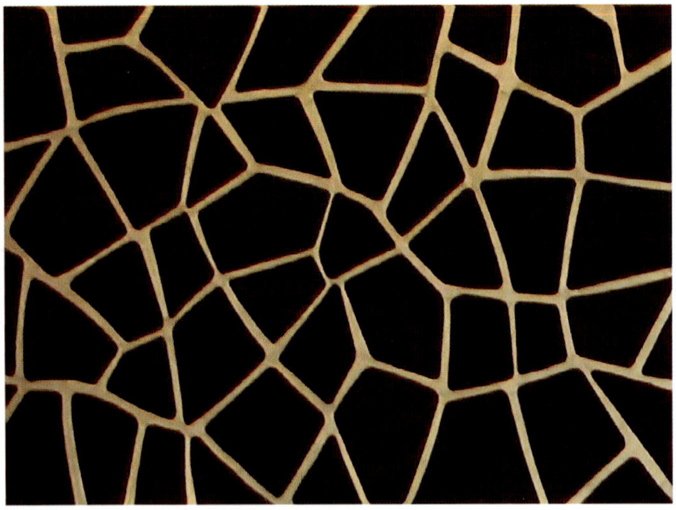

Figures 157a-157b. Animal patterns—classic, timeless, sophisticated, and very popular—can be had in glass tile.
Photo courtesy Mixed-Up-Mosaics

Decorating With Pattern Rules

The best thing about rules is deciding how, when, where, and why to use them; and, how, when, where, and why to break them! Rules are guidelines. Using or not using them in a matter of judgement that grows better with practice.

- The quieter the wall, the busier the floor pattern, *or go with a quiet floor pattern for a hush-hush mood.*
- The bolder the wall pattern, the more gentle the floor, *or make a personal statement with an equally strong floor pattern in a non-competing, quieter color.*
- Use small pattern to make a small room seem spacious, *or enlarge the pattern—but stick with light, bright tiles—to add pizzazz without encroaching.*
- Use a large-scale pattern in a large rooms; *or, use a small-scale pattern in a strong color or a riotous mix of strong colors.*

Remember this: Pattern is a great relief from boredom!

Pattern Underfoot

Glass tile offers the interior designer a seemingly infinite range of possibilities for adding pattern underfoot. Here, for inspiration, are interiors that only hint at the vast quantity of glass tiles available for flooring. Check Chapter 7, Sources for the website addresses of these manufacturers, and be astonished at the wealth of material.

Trend's A Tread of Light Collection in a variety of colors makes possible fascinating carpet-like patterns including a contemporary plaid (Figure 207b). (Patterns of this sort read as soft or strong, depending on the color palette.)

Not all glass tile recommended for bathroom installation is mosaic (1-inch or smaller squares). Orsoni's Polidesign Collection mixes mosaic squares with larger squares and rectangles. Designers can mix-and-match these three sizes and shapes to achieve a variety of plaid, herringbone, brickwork, striped, and other patterns. (See Figures 209a-209e). Interstyle's Trumpet flooring collection includes modular squares and mosaics (Figure 209a).

In addition to mosaic tesserae, Mixed-Up-Mosaics includes glass marbles in its flooring line (Figure 208 and Figure 210). The raised, rounded surface of the marbles provides a massage for bare feet! They can be used alone or to create a decorative path or provide other decorative accents.

Large-format (24 x 24 inches) tiles are also available from some manufacturers, such as Interstyle, Marin Designworks, and others (see Chapter 7, Sources).

Don't forget "ready-made" medallions, like those from Country Floors (Figure 206), which dress up entryways and bathrooms, furnishing any small space with color and pattern.

Figure 158. Mosaic artists Allison Goldenstein and Leslie Provazano, owners of Mixed-Up-Mosaics, direct light bathroom traffic with a curving path of mixed large and small Bubbles. Bubbles glass marble-like tiles provide a gentle massage for bare feet. Bubbles can be used as a contrast with other materials or alone in light-use areas such as small bathroom.
Photo courtesy Mixed-Up-Mosaics

Figure 159. An area rug—worked out meticulously in glass tile—delightfully accessorizes the glass-tile floor and creates all the pattern needed in a unique bathroom. *Photo courtesy Sicis*

Figure 160. Why pile on a wool area rug when a marvelous rug can become part of the overall glass tile design? This captivating floor—area rug and all—is worked out in Sicis' Iridium Collection.
Photo courtesy Sicis

Cavaliere Medallion
60 x 60 in.

Figure 161. It only takes a small amount of glass tile to add enormous style to any floor. Use a glass tile medallion with glass or other materials—wood, stone, or ceramic tile. Country Floors' charming medallion is ready-made.
Photo courtesy Country Floors

Figure 162. Trend named this flooring A Tread of Light, and so it is. Multiple subtle colors of mosaic tile from Patrizia Guci's Scent of Colours Collection for Trend create a sophisticated plaid that works as a wall-to-wall pattern in a London home. This pattern can be beautifully and appropriately scaled for large or small areas.
Photo courtesy Trend

Figure 163. Polidesign glass flooring from Orsoni is a collection of sophisticated patterns, including Polidesign 3, a green and purple plaid with a lustrous surface. Other patterns include an eye-catching herringbone.
Photo courtesy Orsoni

Figures 164a-164b. (opposite and above) Interior Designers John Barman and Kelly Graham created a brilliant glass tile floor—with a medallion sporting a by-the-sea theme—to make the bar/pantry a *must see* for visitors to the Hampton Designer Showhouse at Villa Maria on Mecox Bay.
Photo by Peter Vitale, courtesy John Barman Design/NYC

Chapter 4
Face Value—Finish and Texture

No sooner had clear glass been discovered, than games with glass began as glass makers added color—and more color! (See Chapter 2, Color.) Then clear glass was made more clear—*crystal* clear, adding greater sparkle and a more luxurious look.

Further experimentation added value to the surface or face of glass with ***finishes*** (which affect the look of glass) and ***textures*** (which alter the way glass feels to the touch). These added two design-expanding elements to options in color, sizes, and shapes.

Today, many exciting finishes and textures exist. But, the relative ease with which these can be changed encourages change, making glass the most *fashionable* of all building materials. So, enjoy these, but expect more finishes and textures, keeping forever-young the face of glass tile.

Finishes

Finish varies greatly among tile collections, offering a choice to suit any interior design style. Popular finishes include these, many of which combine texture.

Clear transparent glass—available in countless colors—offers depth, liquidity, and sparkle. Clarity may also differ from collection to collection (Figures 166 and 167a). Color of grout will greatly affect clear glass!

Opaque glass seems to filter light and color, giving it a soft and gentle glow (Figure 165).

Frosted glass gets its look by tumbling (being tossed about with small wood blocks in a contraption that looks like a cement mixer), so that it appears to have been wet and left in the refrigerator to chill. See it in "beach glass" that looks water-tossed and worn (Figure 167b).

Gloss glass has a highly polished shine that, depending on color and pattern, can seem elegantly formal or vivaciously bohemian (Figure 168a).

Matte glass has a softened, dulled look compatible with casual interior design schemes (Figure 168b).

Iridescence, chameleon-like, is a constantly shifting, totally captivating light and color show as colors change with the slightest alteration of light or eye movement. Usually, the surface is silky smooth and very shiny (Figure 169), and luxuriously lustrous, with a mother-of-pearl quality (Figure 170).

Raku iridescence adds to the iridescence light-and-color show a pitted texture based on ancient Japanese raku (Figure 172).

Lunar iridescence adds a rugged 3-D texture to iridescence, heightening emphasis on both (Figure 171).

Crackle adds an antiqued, cracked-surface look to glass tile (Figure 173).

Luster is a very rich molten satin look (Figure 64), adds a substantial, ultra stable look, great for flooring.

Shimmer, a dancing-light effect, animates a wall of glass, even under low-level lighting (Figures 114-116), adding depth and dimension.

Opalesence, a natural-pearl appearance (Figure 125) with tactile appeal.

Metallic finishes give the look of a particular metal to glass (see Color, Metallics, page 29).

Glimmer adds sharp, diamond-bright flecks of light to glass with the addition of natural gemstones and metals (Figure 34a).

Figure 165. The wave-washed, sand-smoothed beach glass finish-by-Nature appearance that gives glass a softened translucency seems reproduced in these tiles from Crossville's Glass Blox Collection. The forty-four colors in the collection include bright solids, natty neutrals, and fashionable blends.
Photo courtesy Crossville

Figure 166. Great clarity gives glass its dazzling liquid look that some describe as "like looking into a deep, clear, sparkling pool."
Photo courtesy Walker Zanger

Figures 167a-167b. Finish makes all the difference between crystal-clear glass (Figure 167a) and frosted glass (Figure 167b) with its opaque diffused-light appearance. Frosted looks are popular backdrops for casual furnishings and unpretentious lifestyles.
Photo courtesy OriginalStyle

Figures 168a-168b. Finish determines whether glass is glossy (Figure 168a) or matte (Figure 168b). High gloss surfaces are generally more formal, while matte surface are at home with casual styles.
Photo courtesy Sandhill Industries

Figure 170. Sicis' Glimmer collection places a lustrous mother-of-pearl iridescent finish over transparent glass, and offers it in twenty-nine indoor/outdoor colors.
Photo courtesy Sicis

Figure 169. (opposite) Iridescence, with its surprising and constantly shifting colors and highly polished look, is always delightful. It is even more so in light, bright colorways like this sunny yellow. There is a broad range of colors available in OriginalStyle's several iridescent collections.
Photo courtesy OriginalStyle

Textures

Texture refers to the actual tactile surface of a material—smooth or rough, even or uneven—qualities that we can feel.

A rooms or interior, of course, doesn't have a *feel, since* inanimate objects cannot feel. What successful interior designs do have is beautifully contrasting textures, materials that encourage touching and feeling, eliciting the emotional responses that we call feelings. These are important in design.

A room boringly furnished with items of same or similar textures—all smooth and even, for example—gets a big boost from even a small amount of textural contrast that results in a sense of dimension with a "please do touch" message.

Like certain wearables (silken fur, gentle cashmere, polished leather, lustrous pearls), some building materials have distinctive, characteristic textures. Think of rough oak beams, finely painted paneling, and brushed stainless steel. Some conjure images of particular decorating periods, styles, and moods.

Glass tile, especially glass mosaic, traditionally has been identified with ancient cathedrals ... but no longer. Contemporary textural treatments make glass tile very versatile and useful to virtually all decorating styles and periods—or at least updated versions of traditional styles in which texture can play a starring role.

Surface charm

The molding process adds texture to the top *(embossing)* and/or of the bottom *(debossing)* of a tile. The result may be a *bas relief* figure like Shells by UltraGlas (Figure 154), or a fabric-inspired look like the ribbed (think of corduroy) tiles by UltraGlas (Figure 184). (Both are also patterns.)

Patterned surface textures may be nature-inspired figures or geometric designs like those by KOG (Figure 180), UltraGlas (Figure 192), and Country Floors' swirl motif from the Paragon collection (Figure 183).

Swarovski STRAS sparkling crystal inlays with their faceted pillow tops that sit above the plane of field tiles in Trend's Topkapi collection by Swiss artist Jasmin Schwitter add texture literally on two levels (Figure 178).

Tile that is tumbled has a slightly gritty, sandpaper-like textured surface that helps to make it skid-proof—a good idea for floors. (See Glass Floors Have Special Textures, page 139)

Marbles (bright and shiny) and pebbles (looking like water-smoothed river rocks) are newer shapes with unique textures that add to the character of a room.

Some looks of texture

Not all tile with a textural look is *texture* by our definition of surface interest. Sometimes, what's underneath the surface conjures images of texture. For example, adding certain patterns to the underside of a tile can result in the look of rough, uneven texture, *leaving the surface smooth and flat*. The advantage is that tiles used as backsplashes—especially cook tops—are subject to splashes of oils and grease, trapping them and making it difficult to clean the surface. These tiles eliminate the problem.

Fancy-looking, multi-dimensional surfaces that could be dust catchers are not a homeowner's fancy. Better a corduroy, brocade, denim, or linen texture that only looks like the real thing.

Certain installations create a sense of texture—important to consider early in the design process. Mosaic blends or gradients, for example, take on an almost tweedy look (Figure 185) in a small bathroom that contrasts richly and warmly with slick mirror.

Making the most of texture

A bathroom with surfaces of varying textures of glass by Marin Designworks (Figure 175) illustrate that texture need not shout to be effective. Texture can be fairly subtle and still make a statement. However, some tile designers and artists are not hesitant in exploring the boundaries.

Mosaic artists Ellen Blakeley (Figure 176) and Lynn Moor (Figure 177) take texture to new dimensions, inspiring a new appreciation for texture as a key design element. Their powerful statements in glass tile have compelling tactile appeal and make it clear that texture is a force that should figure prominently in interior design. The cracklature (cracked surface look) in Ellen Blakeley's work evokes both a surface texture and a sense of infinite depth. Lynn Moore's rugged piece is decidedly heroic—an in-your-face, compelling presence impossible to ignore. Either one in an entryway would make an emphatic statement, setting the tone for interiors to come.

Figure 171. Not all iridescent finishes are highly polished and satin smooth. OriginalStyle's Lunar Collection ups the design ante by combining iridescence with bold texture. Even low-level lighting animates this unique tile amazingly.
Photo courtesy OriginalStyle

Figure 172. GlasTile's Cassandra Rakku Collection is inspired by the ancient raku process that gives glass tiles a densely-textured, pitted surface. Colorways—all with high-sheen metallic iridescence—include gold/silver to blue/purple/green colors, as well as pastel-pearl colorways. This highly reflective tile is effective as a pool surround.
Photo courtesy GlasTile

Figure 173. Trikeenan's Glass Windows Collection tiles have a glass front fused to a ceramic back that gives the tiles a distinctive crackle finish. There is a broad array of colors and patterns in the collection.
Photo courtesy Trikeenan Tileworks

Figure 174. Walker Zanger's Weave glass tile is a collection of four styles and nine mosaic patterns. Each of the eight colors in the collection have an iridescent finish that adds dash wherever it is used—indoors for interest, or outdoors as an exciting border for the pool.
Photo courtesy Walker Zanger

Designing With Texture

Texture is important in all styles and places, but is especially important in:

- Rooms with monochromatic color schemes typical of Contemporary rooms (Figure 6b).
- Interiors with rustic looks that demand strong textural contrasts.
- Any area where a distinct mood needs to be underscored, such as the high-glamour, ultra-feminine bath/dressing room (Figure 61), which needs polish, shimmer, and sheen. Or, the boldly textured garden wall (Figure 14) fits glass tile smartly against the wall material surrounding it and with plants and furnishings.

Glass Floors Have Special Textures

Floors, because they are a large and very visible part of any interior, deserve serious design attention. Probably the first question a designer asks is what material to use? The answer: A practical material—one with a safe (non-skid) surface, that is strong, durable, easily maintained, and beautiful!

Glass is that material.

• Are glass tiles safe?

Yes, thanks to *texture*, a plus in other tiles, a *must* in floor tiles. A non-skid texture is manufactured into the surface of glass tile. Additionally, some manufacturers recommend applying special non-skid coatings or finishes—especially if tiles are installed in a wet area (shower stall, bathroom, entry hall, and so on).

• What does this special non-skid texture look like?

First of all, although skid-proofing sounds utilitarian, these surfaces are attractive. UltraGlas adds bas-relief patterns to glass, like Squiggles on the high-tech looking stair treads in Figure 190. Some tiles have a sandpaper-like texture that increases what manufacturers describe as a coefficient of friction (think of well-designed car tire treads that ensure grip on a wet pavement).

• Is glass floor tile strong?

Yes. Glass flooring complies with strict commercial and residential building codes. Additionally, glass slabs used for "bridge-like" walkways seen in contemporary architecture (Figure 189) is custom manufactured and site-specific (see Glass Tile Inspirations for Kitchens and Baths, Chapter 5). Glass floor tiles are stronger and thicker than wall tiles, which must not be used as flooring! Sicis' NeoGlas collection, for example, is ¼-inch thick. Appropriate substrates and installation techniques and material ensure that glass floor tiles will not crack. (See page 172)

• How practical, easy to maintain, is glass flooring?

Very! It stands up to the wear and tear of heavily trafficked commercial facilities, whose management is very conscious of holding down cleaning costs. Find tile flooring by Mixed-Up-Mosaic in busy casino lobbies in Las Vegas and Connecticut. The same mosaic tile from Sicis' Iridium Collection used in a large commercial site in South Africa stands up to high foot traffic and is submerged for special events! Iridium is recommended for residential use (Figure 158). Manufacturers may recommend particular cleaning materials, but usually a damp mop is all that's needed to keep these floors sparkling.

• Is glass flooring beautiful?

The most obvious thing about glass is its glowing beauty that *begins* life with a luminous patina that it takes other materials years to develop. Its luster is unparalleled. This is evident in the Bisazza mosaic tile floor of Gianfranco Ferre's E'SPA in Milan (see Figure 34a), which incorporates many hues of chocolate and espresso browns highlighted with gold flecks.

See it in glass tile used as an element in medallions, borders, or runners enlivening natural stone floors in elegant traditional designs by Marc-Michael Interiors (Figures 2-4).

The unique beauty of glass is visible in a dazzling red-coral and seashell medallion in designer John Barman's butler pantry floor at a Hamptons Designer Showcase (Figures 164a-164b). The floor design established the theme of the room and paid homage to the bayside setting of the historic house.

• What kinds of designs are possible?

With the myriad sizes, shapes, textures, finishes, patterns, and colors, think of "designs unlimited." For examples, see "Pattern Underfoot," Chapter 3, Pattern.

Figure 175. Marin Designworks' custom glass tiles and matching knobs with a highly-polished sheen, custom glass countertop, and a unique color-coordinated glass vessel in lieu of a standard sink add up to an artfully designed bathroom.
Photo Marin Designworks

Figure 176. A glass tile with metal leaf and black crackle finish gives the tile tremendous depth and a sense of infinite mystery. This work of art beautifully shows mosaic artist Ellen Blakeley's dramatic signature shattered-glass mosaic style.
Photo courtesy Ellen Blakeley Studios

Figure 177. Color plays second fiddle to exaggerated texture in this extraordinarily harmonious fine-art work by noted mosaic artist Lynn Moor.
Photo courtesy Lynn Moor

Figure 178. Textural interest is intensified by combining and contrasting tiles of different textures. Swiss artist Jasmine Schwitter pits three different textures against one another. Vitreo (semitransparent), Brillante (transparent glass with veins of enamel and avventurina stone), and Swarovski's STRASS crystal tiles create a continuing and lively artistic conversation. (It is easy to lower the volume by reducing the degree of contrast.)
Photo courtesy Trend

Figure 179. Arroyo by UltraGlas is one of seventeen distinctively-textured floor tiles that can be combined with standard colors or patterns by UltraGlas.
Photo courtesy UltraGlas

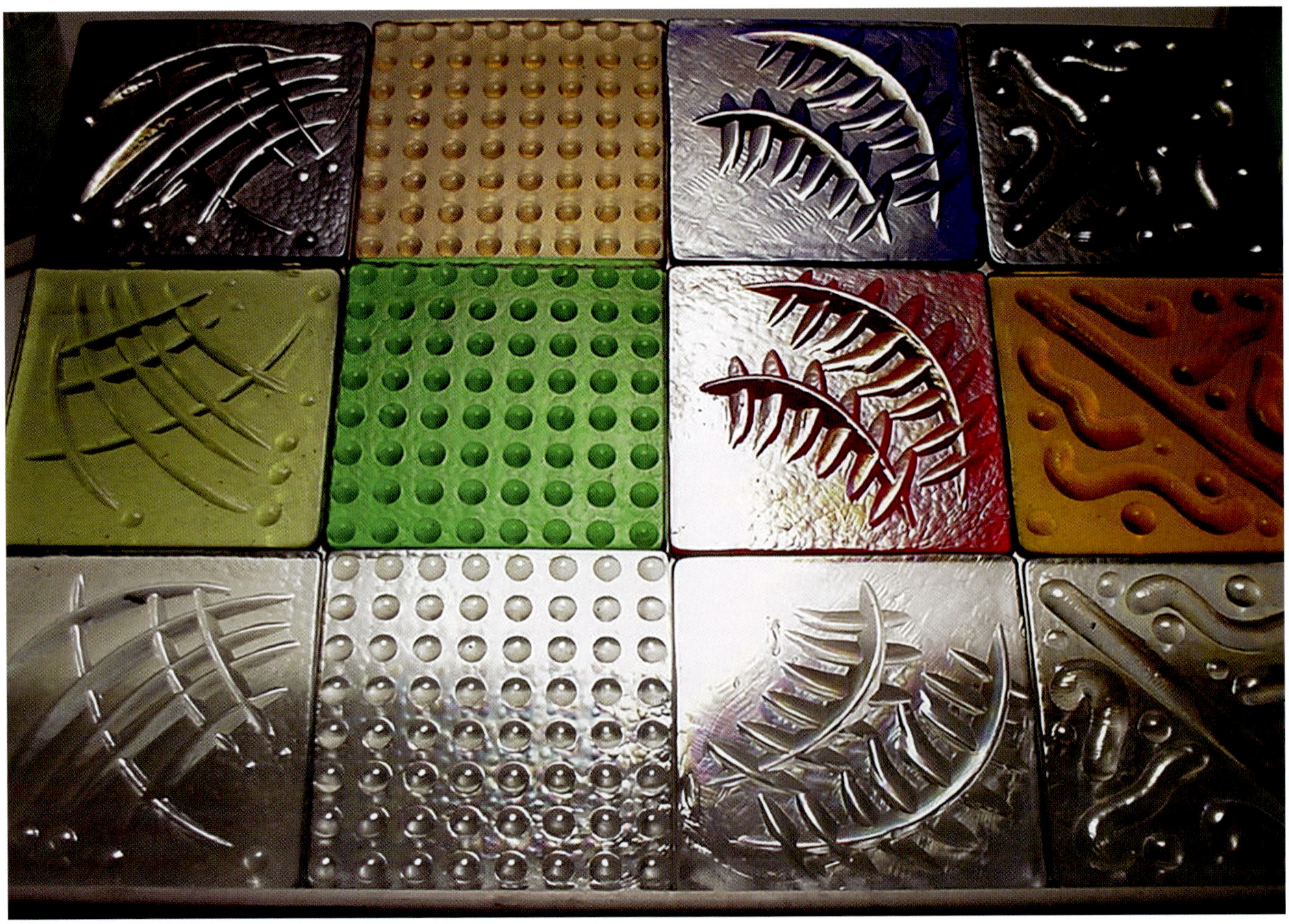

Figure 180. Textural variety is the thing at KOG, America's oldest art glass manufacturer. Shown is a sampling of the company's art-inspired Art Glass Wall Tile collection. These and other textures are available in various patterns, colors, and shapes. KOG, famous for its custom work, will custom cut Art Glass Wall tile.
Photo courtesy KOG Hot Glass Studio

Figure 181. UltraGlas specializes in glass tiles in a variety of unique textures in thirty-one different lead-free opaque or translucent colors. Here Group Warm—tiles is a warm color range sampling—shows what a difference texture makes.
Photo courtesy UltraGlas

Figure 182. Chrystal tile gets its watery, prismatic, highly textured crinkled silk appearance from layering over 24-carat gold leaf with clear glass in the proprietary Marin Designwork way.
Photo courtesy Marin Designwork

Figure 183. The Paragon Series from Country Floors is available in a number of colors, finishes—silver and copper foil backing, colored glass thread, or embedded industrial metal pieces—and designs that create distinctive sculptural textural effects.
Photo courtesy Country Floors

Figure 184. Textures often take on the look of a fabric. Here, Ribbed by UltraGlas has the look of a handsomely whaled (ribbed) corduroy. UltraGlas places some textural designs on the underside of easy-to-clean flat glass surface in a technique called debossing. Flat glass is good for installations in kitchens where grease from frying food is deposited on walls. More dimensional embossed patterns feature motifs on the outside of the tile in bas- or high relief. It is ideal for bathroom installation.
Photo courtesy UltraGlas

Figure 185. The seemingly random array of different colored tessera—like that in Trend's Lux collection in this contemporary bathroom—creates tactile interest, a design ploy that works especially well in a small space where pattern might encroach.
Photo courtesy Trend

Figure 187. For 2005 Jundial Décor showcase, architects João Benassi and Rafael Bernassi warm up the floor and highlight the wall with Vidrotil glass tile in a medley of exciting colors that add the excitement and welcome.
Photo courtesy Vidrotil

Figure 188. Glass tile flooring offers a visual depth that no other material matches. Interstyle's Parade glass floor tile is available in a number of series that offer options in colors. Every floor conceivably can be a custom design thanks to the myriad of textures, patterns, sizes, and shapes. Shown here is the Trumpet collection that mixes modular tiles.
Photo courtesy Interstyle Ceramic & Glass Tile

Figure 186. (opposite) Brazilian architect Lia Carbonati uses a blend of Vidrotil Medley ¾-inch mosaic glass tile in two colors to add refined texture and warmth to the walls of a sophisticated interior. Finely grouted line underscores the elegance of the warmly-colored tile.
Photography by Martin Szmick, courtesy of the architect and Vidrotil

Figure 189. Glass flooring is strong, durable, light-transmitting, compatible with contemporary design, and non-skid when properly textured and finished. Hauser Architects specified UltraMatte surface texture for the glass flooring for a suspended bridge. The glass flooring is made by laminating 3/8-in. clear tempered UltraGlas to 3/8-in. clear tempered flat glass with a frosted interliner. UltraGlas makes glass flooring in seventeen different textures. The glass tile maker recommends a non-slip coating for wet environments.
Photo courtesy Hauser Architects, San Francisco, CA

Figure 190. UltraSquiggle glass flooring by UltraGlas was specified by Hauser Architects for stair treads that make for a lighter, brighter stairwell. As an added safety measure, UltraGlas recommends a non-slip coating for installations in wet environments. UltraGlas glass flooring is designed to meet or exceed coefficient of friction codes demanded for safety. It may be specified in any one of seventeen textures, sixteen color patterns, or thirty-one standard solid colors. Glass tile—right for traditional and contemporary houses—may combine textures, patterns, and colors.
Photo courtesy Hauser Architects, San Francisco, CA

Figure 191. Marble-like Bubbles contrast texturally with other glass, ceramic, stone, or metal tiles, but can be used alone in light-use areas such as small bathroom.
Photo courtesy Mixed-Up-Mosaics

Figure 192. Large-format glass tile from Interstyle's Cello series add a contemporary note and transparent color to the floor.
Photo courtesy Interstyle Ceramic & Glass Tile

Figure 193. Floors may wear the same tile as walls in certain cases. Here, Brazilian Architect Lia Carbonati covers surfaces in a cross-stitch design of ¾-inch mosaics in Vidrotil color numbers 1500, 3700, and 7001.
Photography by Martin Szmick, courtesy of the architect and Vidrotil

Figure 193a. Floors created by Marin Designworks are the dazzling focal point of any room. This one features Mahogany Hammered-textured glass tile cut into filigree designs that enliven the background of Pistachio-Onyx tile. This one welcomes guest to TJ's Steakhouse at the Hilton Hotel in Las Vegas. The design is a sure thing for residences, too.

Chapter Five
Sizes and Shapes

Part of the pleasure of designing with glass tile is an abundance of sizes, shapes, and trim pieces that make it possible to achieve any style.

Recognizing historic and popular styles—and knowing the tile *sizes and shapes* that underscore them—is a good place to start the design process. This knowledge speeds up adopting a style and *selecting* the tiles for a project. For inspiration, here is a list of popular conventional styles in this book. Tiles chosen by interior designers to achieve these distinctive looks warrant close looks.

- **Traditional** style, based on historic European (mainly English and French) periods, is familiar, refined, comforting, and timeless. *Generally, mid-size tiles for walls and all-tile floors carry off this look, but working small jewel-like mosaic glass tile into a traditional floor medallion works beautifully. (Figure 2)*

- **Contemporary** interiors call for clean architectural lines, light (sometimes bright) colors, and no clutter. *Tile size choices are extreme—small or large. Small mosaic covers a contemporary living room wall seamlessly (Figures 6a), page 00. It's light color and refractive surface adds to the floating feeling of a sky-high condominium. Large-format tiles for walls and floors are very Contemporary.*

- **Old World** looks recall Mediterranean influences, demanding strong vivid colors and generous scale. *Often large-scale patterns with Moorish or other Mediterranean motifs are made of mosaic tiles. The kitchen hood by Marc-Michaels is an excellent example (Figure 4).*

- **Rustic** looks (Southwestern, Mid-Western, or New England) call to mind dark, heavy timbers and snug interiors. *Midsize tiles in deep, strong colors and matte or tumbled finishes are at home here (see Figure 81). So are small mosaics that appear embedded in rough-plaster walls (Figure 215). Of course, there are exceptions to every rule, so look at Figure 94, a Pennsylvania bathroom with massive timbers and deep blue, shiny mosaic walls!*

- **Asian** influences are in a bedroom with shoji screens, a low-lying bed, and a strong emphasis on an essentials-only sensitivity. *A screening wall of translucent glass mosaic tiles heightens the sense of mystery and romance. (Figure 34b)*

- **Romantic** interiors are frankly feminine. *What could be more appropriate in a woman's bath/dressing room than glimmering mosaic tile in fashionable Schiaparelli-inspired Hot Pink? Size? As long as tiles are not huge (and manly), tile size is less important than color, texture, and pattern. (Figure 61)*

- **Beach** houses are so mood-making that the look is popular even in the heart of the city. *Tiles that underscore the beach theme are not-too-big squares or rectangles that look as though they had been tumbled by the sea and washed on shore by a benevolent tide. (Figure 84)*

- **Eclectic** interior design is not a mixed-up hodgepodge, but a deliberate design that simultaneously strongly contrasts and unites two seemingly opposed design elements. *An example is placing ornate Period furniture against a sleek mosaic glass-tile wall with an urbane, over-scaled, stylized version of an antique textile pattern. (Figure 39 and Figure 92)*

- **Tropical** looks are based largely on jungle-like floral motifs. *They are usually worked out in colorful mosaic tiles that can be fine (polished) for interiors, or rustic (matte) for exteriors. (Figure 16)*

- **Glamorous** looks call for over-the-edge glitter and the kind of extreme confidence that places a brilliant gold fireplace against a fire-engine red wall. *This red wall and the smart curved lines of a fireplace mantel completely sheathed in 24-karat gold mosaic fill the bill (Figure 9)!*

- **Modern** interiors feature clean lines and sophisticated colors—often with a bit of quiet flash and dash. *Gold-flecked mosaic tile gives this floor its flawless, seamless, ultra polished look. (Figure 33)*

- **Personal.** When no conventional "name" style or look will do, the only course left is to trust oneself, choose the things that make your heart beat faster, and create your own unique design. It's possible to find inspiration in many interiors in this book, take bits and pieces from each, and build a look you love, *using the tile size or sizes that's just right for your Personal Style. (Please do send us a photo of your completed Personal Style room!)*

Figure 194. Walls, floors, and ceiling all wear the same size glass mosaic in a design that thoughtfully lays floor mosaic on a non-static, out-of-the-box diagonal and creates a statement-making border with an updated antique Greek wave motif.
Photo courtesy Oceanside Glasstile

Figure 195. GlasTile's Block Party collection preview board shows designers at-a-glance a myriad options in mix-and-match sizes, shapes, patterns (confetti), and colors. Colorways include solids and combo solids—that result from fusing multi-colors as liners and squares. A choice of multicolor squares includes a random, scattered look or precise mini squares fused into one larger square. Block Party is also available in Pastel, Florida, Neutral, and custom color combinations.
Photo courtesy GlasTile

Figures 196a-196b. (right and opposite) These two baths demonstrate that even when working in the same or a similar color palette you can achieve entirely unique designs. Interstyle's Watercolors collection is composed of translucent, satin matte finished tiles in twenty-four different loose tile sizes, fifty-five different colors, and four mesh-mounted mosaic tiles.
Photos courtesy Interstyle Ceramic & Glass Tile

Figure 197. Sicisbricks are transparent glass blocks covered in Glimmer mosaics, transparent glass with iridescent pearlized surfaces. They are available in the three shapes and sizes, as shown. They come in Blackurrant (bright blue), Apple (green), and Strawberry (red). These innovative glass bricks (or blocks) make it easy to create a room divider or partition that admits modulated light. Beautiful in natural daylight, Sicisbricks are especially effective when romantically backlit.
Photo courtesy Sicis

Sizes

A variety of sizes makes scaling a design to a particular room and installation in architecturally awkward spaces less complicated. Most manufacturers offer several different collections in a wide range of standard sizes (for quick delivery). These tiles are as small as ¾-inch mosaic squares and as large as 24-inch x 24-inch (large format) tiles. One-inch mosaic tiles are an amazingly flexible design tool, moving easily between antique, historic, traditional, and contemporary styles.

Large-format (12x12-inch or 24x24-inch) tiles are contemporary, but also work well in traditional baths and kitchens, depending on color and texture (Figure 192).

Between extreme small and large sizes are familiar 3-inch x 3-inch, 4-inch x 4-inch, and other "medium range" sizes most frequently seen in kitchens and bathrooms.

Many manufacturers also make custom sizes (which take longer to produce and deliver). Some *specialize* in custom work. Architectural Glass, Inc. in Beacon, New York, for instance, is one of the older glass tile studios in North America. It can produce custom three-dimensional shapes to conform to columns, cornices and other architectural features as may be required in restoration work or desired for luxury building. Other custom specialists include Artistic Tile, Mixed-Up-Mosaics, Marin Designworks, and KOG.

Shapes

Shapes vary. The most familiar field or ground (background) tile shapes are squares, rectangles, diamonds, and long, narrow listelli and other trim pieces. Newer shapes abound. Here are some:

- Pebbles, ancient stone shapes, (Figure 200)
- Marbles, large and small, (Figures 191 and Figure 205b)
- Penny Rounds, (Figure 211)
- Circles, Ovals, Running Ribbons, (Figure 137a)
- Quilt shapes, (Figure 30)
- Irregular square and rectangle shapes, (Figure 213b)
- Free-form, nature-inspired shapes, (Figures 21 and 205a).

Tile shapes are also becoming more three-dimensional, adding strong surface interest. Trend, for example, makes a faceted, jewel-like, crystal mini-square to accent field tiles. Because of their strong tactile interest, see them in Chapter 5, Texture (Figure 178).

Varying sizes and shapes to heighten interest

Variety, the spice of life, adds intrigue. Even when a tile design project is limited to same-size tiles, variety is easy enough to achieve; but freedom to use a few or many different sizes and shapes makes design child's play. Here are examples and inspiration.

Designing with same-size, same-shape tiles

- Lay same-size tiles in different directions or patterns. In the bath in Figure 194, floor tiles laid on the diagonal add contrasting line to walls and ceiling plus a space-expanding sense of movement. (The stylized Greek-wave motif border uses same-size tiles cut-to-fit, but contrasting colors necessarily define the design.)
- Instead of a simple grid, install brick-shaped tiles in a herringbone pattern (Figure 203).
- Install one or more rows of brick-shaped tiles vertically to creates a border for a wall of tiles laid in a herringbone pattern or horizontal grid (Figure 202).
- Create a zigzag/herringbone border (Figure 204)
- Instead of a simple grid pattern, stagger rows of square or rectangular tiles in what bricklayers call a Flemish bond, eliminating straight grout lines and creating a more interesting pattern. An attention-getting broad panel behind a tub is achieved in this way—made more dramatic with contrasting color tiles. (Figure 206)

Mixing sizes and shapes

A basic grid pattern that simply stacks tiles in orderly rows (Figure 96) is key to the serene mood in this kitchen; but two rows of narrow liner bars create a border that adds interest and maintains the mood.

Mixing modularly sized tiles makes for tremendous variety and many companies offer them. Trend's Liberty collection in the red kitchen (Figure 210) shows how effective this technique is. Interstyle offers compositions of modulars, and two bathrooms with Interstyle's modular tiles clearly demonstrate how looks vary, even when designers work in the same color palette. (Figures 196a-196b).

Mixing sizes and shapes to mimic familiar basketry, textile, and other patterns surprises and delights. Crossville's basket weave pattern is one (see Figure 201). The dynamic herringbone, a men's wear pattern, (Figures 202-204) is another. Installing liner-bars vertically—and staggering contrasting colors—achieves a fame-stitch pattern in a blue-and-white bath (Figure 199).

Designs possible with different sizes and shapes seem delightfully endless. (See Chapter 3, Pattern)

Figure 198. Glass tile at its most simple—clear glass in popular sizes and shapes and great colors—gives designers ample opportunity for creative design. In this case, a positive (light background) panel of smaller tiles in a checkerboard pattern is surrounded by a negative (dark) background of larger tiles. The visual play between sizes and shapes is fascinating. The total effect is riveting.
Photo courtesy OriginalStyle

Figure 199. Ann Sacks' Lake Garda collection offers interior designers a wide range of sizes and shapes, as well as colors, in coordinating wall and floor tiles. Here are 1x8 inch tiles in six different colors installed vertically in the shower stall and on the tub surround. Promenade, a 6x12-inch field glass tile in surf gloss—in a watery blue-green—covers the floor. Recommended for light traffic areas, the flooring comes in forty matte colors and sizes ranging from 2x2 inches to 12x12 inches.
Photo courtesy Ann Sacks

Figure 200. Combining two different sizes and shapes—each in different colors and textures—ups the design ante. Marin Designwork's Reno border combines Pebble tessera with cobalt blue hammered glass tile to create maximum interest in a relatively small area.
Photo courtesy Marin Designworks

Figure 201. Small mosaics, small mini-brick-like rectangles, squares, and liner bars in Crossville's Glass Blox collection (along with forty-four colors) make possible a variety of imaginative pattern designs. Here, a scaled up basket weave pattern with dynamic diagonal movement transforms what could have been a mundane cabinet base into an arresting work of art.
Photo courtesy Crossville

Figure 202. The Neopolis collection from Country Floors is available in several different sizes and shapes that lend themselves to designer statements. Here, a dynamic herringbone pattern is capped by rectangular, brick-shaped tiles that create a handsome border.
Photo courtesy Country Floors

Figure 204. A ready-made herringbone border adds an interesting contrast in size and shapes of tiles in Rosan Imports *Fantastiques* collection.
Photo courtesy Rosan Imports

Figure 203. Slender brick-shaped tiles form mosaic artist Erin Adams' unique herringbone pattern for Erin Adams Design, distributed exclusively by Ann Sacks.
Photo courtesy Ann Sacks

Figures 205a-205b. Bedrock Industries makes all its glass products from 100 percent recycled glass. The company produces a fascinating color palette in a wide variety of special shapes and popular sizes. Included are circles, squares, rectangles, pebbles, teardrops, and listelli in "breadstick" (long and skinny) and "hushpuppie" (small, cute) sizes, plus imaginative freeform shapes like those that accent this kitchen backsplash and border.
Photo courtesy Bedrock Industries

Figure 206. To achieve both variety and unity, interior designs often mix various sizes of tiles from the same collection. Here, larger tiles in several of the twenty available colors from Walker Zanger's Spa Glass collection create an arresting focal point behind the tub, while smaller tessera in the same color blend add sparkle and unifying texture to the tub surround.
Photo courtesy Walker Zanger

Figures 207a-207b. The Roku collection by Walker Zanger, a translucent glass tile, is inspired by Eastern aesthetics that work well with contemporary American design. In addition to various sizes and shapes, the Roku collection is available in six colors and a choice of matte or metallic finish.
Photo courtesy Walker Zanger

Figure 208. Mosaic tile designer Karen Story's Jewel Stone collection is made of shimmering colored glass cut into "chiclet-sized" pieces, then kiln-fired to soften the edges and arranged in colorful combinations. Mesh-mounted for easy installation, Jewel Stone strips may be used alone or combined with Jewel Stone liners as borders. They are great accents for field tiles from other collections.
Photo courtesy Dolce Glass Tile

Mixing and Matching Sizes

Not all tiles are equal—some are thicker than others! Mixing different-thickness tiles of any material creates a problem for the installer who must create a surface with a flat plane (important for walls, critical for floors!) While installers can deal with the problem when working with ceramic tile (add more mud), compensating for different thicknesses of glass tile is far more difficult. Avoid potential problems—be aware:

- Tiles from the same collection of a manufacturer have similar thickness and can be worked into a smooth-surfaced pattern.
- Tiles from different collections or manufacturers may have different thicknesses.
- Glass tiles may differ in thickness with tiles in other materials (ceramic, stone, or metal). To successfully mix glass and stone tiles, check out sources such as Artistic Tile, which mesh-mounts (on large sheets) mixtures of these two materials in uniform thicknesses.
- When mixing any glass tiles—from different collections by the same manufacturer, different manufacturers, or with different materials—consult your installer before placing your order.

Concept Boards—what a concept!

Concept boards, which demonstrate possible tile combinations, are a great boon to designers. These boards, sometimes called Preview Boards, cut through the clutter in the tile showroom, help the designer to focus, and speed the design process. Here are several Concept Boards created by tile designer Rudy Santos, owner of Rosan Imports, indicated in crisp black and white many possible combinations of tiles from his Fantastiques Collection.

(Figures 209a-209e)

Figures 209a-209e. (Above and following two pages) Unless one designs tiled walls and floors every day, the task can seem daunting. Where to start? With a concept or preview board that means to inspire by showing some possibilities. Rosan Imports' Concept Boards combine various shapes and sizes of glass tile, black marble, mother-of-pearl, and metal tessera (field tiles) and listelli (narrow border trim) in ways that are easily grasped and built upon.
Photos courtesy Rosan Imports

MCB-052

MCB-054

MCB-051

MCB-053

Figure 210. A variety of sizes and shapes in the Liberty collection by Trend adds enormous visual appeal, while allowing the designer to stick to one unifying color such as this Tiffany red. Choices of a range of sizes and shapes also make it easier to design around such obstacles as architectural elements—such as doors and windows—and furnishings like cabinets and shelves which are especially prevalent in kitchens.
Photo courtesy Trend

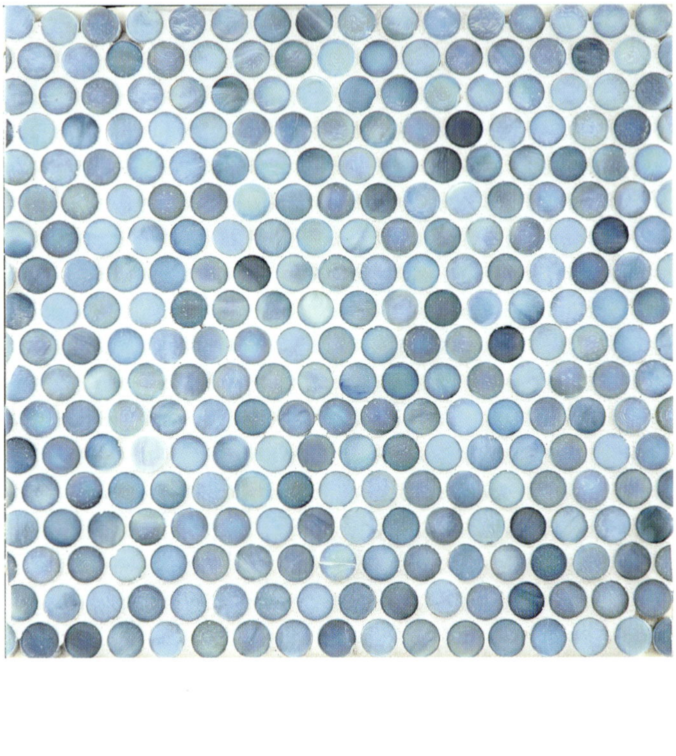

Figure 211. Ann Sacks, the trend-setting source for remarkable wall and floor surfacing materials, recreated a venerable ceramic tile shape—penny rounds. Glace Pennies ¾-inch rounds glass mosaic tile reminiscent of tiles used in the New York City Subway. Glace Sticks, a 1x6-inch stacked, brick-shaped tile, coordinates with Glace Pennies. Glace—with its distinctive smoky, quartz-like iridescence is sold netted for easy installation and works for walls and floors.
Photo courtesy Ann Sacks

Figure 212. Mixed-Up-Mosaics listelli—thin bar commonly used as liners or trim—become uncommon fine art in the hands of a clever designer. Do a whole wall or create a mural.
Photo courtesy Mixed-Up-Mosaics

Figures 213a-213b. Irregularly shaped tiles offer interior designers new opportunities for expression. Erin Adams' tiles add big-city sophistication to a bathroom in a Kips Bay Designer Showcase house (Figure 213a), while Interstyle's River Crystals border adds spice to a kitchen wall.
Photos courtesy Erin Adams Designs (Figure 213a) and Interstyle Ceramic & Glass Tile (Figure 213b)

Figure 214. Modular collections—different sized tiles that fit together to form squares or rectangles—offer unlimited possibilities. Choose between a soothing monochromatic palette and mix-and-match colors for a livelier look.
Photo courtesy Interstyle Ceramic & Glass Tile

Figure 215. Small mosaic offer tremendous versatility, especially when they're available in a wide range of mix-and-match color palettes called blends or gradients. Color weighting—determining how to distribute dark and light values—influences a design. Spacing like this seemingly random placement adds a handcrafted look to a Southwestern style home.
Photo courtesy Interstyle Ceramic & Glass Tile

Figure 215a. Marin Designworks contrasts Carat Satin-textured glass in a vanity countertop with a ribbon-like swirl of Sonoma Green Wave glass. An undulating 24-Carat Wave glass ribbon cut into white tiles add interest to the backsplash. The result: a bath that makes a real splash!
Photo courtesy Marin Designworks

Figure 215b. Marin Designworks is noted for its custom designs that combine unique cuts of glass. Here, Oceana Wave textured glass is cut into the mirror and limestone slab, adding a cohesive water-wave design element that makes this bathroom unique.
Photo courtesy Marin Designworks

Chapter 6
Installing Glass Tile

Architects, designers, and homeowners beware!

Installing glass tile, like working with fine jewelry, requires expert knowledge, skills, and tools. Not all tile installers have these. Because glass tile is an ***unforgiving***, relatively expensive material, those buying glass tile for a design project should be aware of these "glass tile installation basics." Then, interview and see an actual installation by the installer you are considering hiring!

Issues and Options

- Substrates. All glass tiles need the proper substrate. All wet areas such as a kitchen backsplash, bathroom, and glass tile floors need a cement-based substrate for moisture control. Glass flooring requires a stable substrate.
- Membranes. The right membrane must be placed under glass tile. Overly compressive membranes cause glass tile to crack, and using membranes with thin-set (not a thick mud) mortar can cause curing problems. Some membranes do not work with certain backings on glass mosaic, which include face/paper-mounted, dot-mounted, and mesh-mounted.
- Mortar and grout. Choices are important, since they affect color. Dark thin-set mortars tend to dull glass mosaic colors, while white thin-set mortars make translucent and transparent mosaics appear brighter. Any color grout will impart some color to the glass.

Working with Glass Tile

Arthur Mintie, Director of Technical Services at Laticrete International, a leading supplier of installation materials, is a recognized authority on installation techniques and materials. Here he shares his own expertise, and mentions specific Laticrete® materials that he recommends. (Please bear in mind that manufacturers supply specific materials to use and how best to install their tiles; such guidelines should be heeded.)

Glass is impervious. Which means there is no *tooth* or porous surface like ceramic tile has for adhesive to sink into and stick to. So glass requires good mortar mixing and mortar spreading techniques, and consistent and accurate tile placement. Glass tiles require a thin-set mortar with tenacious bond strength. Most installers have had bad experiences with glass tiles losing bond and coming loose, generally because they did not use a quality latex fortified Portland cement mortar. Simple dry-set mortars and most low-end, multi-purpose thin-set mortars do not have the bond strength to ensure a good grip to the glass surface. For glass, only the best will do.

For bathrooms, showers, countertops, and other areas where water damage can occur near or below the tile application, installers should use a waterproofing membrane such as Laticrete® 9235 Waterproofing Membrane or Laticrete® Hydroban waterproofing underneath the tile installation. Consult with the manufacturer of the tile installation materials for a compatible waterproofing membrane system for the building's substrate, which may consist of a number of different materials.

Two Methods for Installing Glass Mosaic

There are two methods for installing glass mosaics. The one-step method is suitable over masonry type surfaces including paper-faced mosaics. The two-step method is suggested for large tile and mesh-backed mosaics.

The one-step method uses a mix of a unique latex thin-set and grout. Laticrete® 4237 Latex Additive mixed with Laticrete® Sanded Grout 1500 Series (color to be selected) is one possible mix. Use this method for masonry type surfaces.

If the glass mosaics are paper-face mounted, installers may use the one-step method of installation. Most glass mosaic in the past was paper-face mounted. Working with paper-faced tiles requires more skill and accuracy than back dot-mounted or rear mesh-mounted.

In this method, the thin-set mortar should be spread on the substrate with a 3/16" square notch trowel. Additional thin-set mortar is combed onto the backs of the tile sheets, in effect filling the grout joints with the thin-set mortar. Using a liquid latex thin-set mortar designed for this purpose, contractors should mix in a sanded grout and use this combination as a *colored* thin-set mortar. The tile sheets should be placed into the freshly spread thin-set mortar, spread onto the surface, and tapped into place with a beating block or rubber grout float. Once the tiles have reached an initial set, the paper facing should be peeled off. After the tiles have set firmly, the same colored mortar should be used to touch up grout joints where sheets meet, imperfections are found, and pinholes exist.

The conventional two-step method is used for large format glass tiles, rear mesh-mounted, and paper-face mounted glass mosaic tiles. Spread the high performance polymer fortified thin-set mortar (e.g. Laticrete 254 Platinum), white in color, using a 3/16-inch square notch trowel onto the substrate and flatten the trowel ridges to a uniform adhesive layer. Next, back-butter the tiles with additional mortar. Carefully set the tile or sheets into place and tap with a beating block or rubber grout float. For paper face-mounted tiles, peel off the paper when the tiles reach an initial set. Once the tiles are set firmly in place, tiles can be grouted in the normal fashion.

For both methods, installers should be as accurate as possible in placing the tiles. (Rear mesh-mounted tiles are more forgiving in that they can be more easily adjusted if necessary.)

Technique for Installing Glass Tiles

Use high-quality latex fortified thin-set mortar. Generally, a white thin-set works for many applications. Do not build up the thin-set mortar more than a 1/8-inch thickness. If the surface needs to be corrected, apply a skim coat of the latex fortified thin-set mortar to correct any deficiencies. Do not build up the thin-set mortar greater than a ¼-inch per lift. Allow the skim coat to harden for a minimum of 72 hours at 70 degrees F prior to installing the tiles. Clean the backs of the tiles and wipe dry. Do not install the glass tiles if they are wet. Spread the thin-set mortar using a notch trowel to ensure maximum coverage. Back-trowel the tiles with additional thin-set mortar to ensure that the mortar trowel lines do not show through the glass tiles. The tiles should be tapped into place using a rubber grout float or a beating block.

For larger format glass tiles, layout can make the difference in the final appearance. Spread out the work on the floor to visualize the finished job. Layouts will minimize the number of cuts ultimately made. The more full tiles one sees, the better the outcome of the installation.

Grouting Glass Tiles

For best performance in all types of installations, an epoxy grout is recommended. Epoxy grout will create a grout joint as dense and easy to clean as the glass itself. Note that epoxy grout can only be used in the conventional two-step method of tile installation. Epoxy grout is best for wet area applications such as bathrooms and kitchens. Laticrete® SpectraLock™ Pro Grout offers superior results. However, consult with the glass tile manufacturer for their thoughts on compatibility with epoxy grouts.

Installers can also use a non-sanded or sanded grout depending on the grout joint texture desired. The smoother texture of non-sanded grouts looks more sophisticated while the rougher texture of sanded grouts looks more rustic. Note that most sanded grouts will achieve higher strengths than non-sanded grouts, a fact worth considering when choosing grout. Either Laticrete® Sanded Grout 1500 Series or Laticrete® UnSanded Grout 1600 Series mixed with Laticrete® 1776 Grout Enhancer is recommended. Use an unsanded grout if the glass potentially could be scratched.

Cutting Mosaic and Glass Tiles

Installing glass tile and mosaic calls for cutting glass products using the proper tools and techniques. A good installer should have an array of conventional tools for use on many larger sized glass tiles and a set of special tools for mosaic. Cutting mosaic requires two special tools:

- Glass mosaic tile nippers – this double-wheeled special nipper has cutting wheels on each nipper arm to enable it to cut through glass neatly and accurately.
- A 3/16" square notch trowel – this hard-to-find trowel is great for installing glass mosaics but may have to be special-ordered.

To cut glass mosaic, use a glass mosaic tile nipper. The nipper makes accurate cuts, ensuring straight edges and a proper fit. To cut larger format glass tiles, use the following cutting and fitting guidelines:

- Corners. Nip with glass tile nippers. The double-wheeled nippers make clean, precise, sharp cuts.
- Drilling. Use a wet drill process to make holes in high quality glass tile.
- Edge Finishing. Use a rubbing stone or Dremel® rotating electric sanding and smoothing device to produce a finished edge.
- L-shaped cuts. Use a marble diamond bit (i.e., 5" wheel) on an electric hand grinder. Put masking tape over cutting line to minimize chipping.
- Straight cuts. Score and snap with a hand cutter such as a newer 8 mm carbide wheel housed in a ball bearing casing. Apply the *least* amount of pressure to score the tile. Glass tile breaks from the heat generated from the carbide wheel, not from the force used. The lighter the score, the better the snap.
- Water jet. Using a wet saw may result in chipping of the top and bottom of the tile, irregular edging, and some color loss. Wet saws are not generally recommended for cutting high quality glass because high quality glass tile has a breaking strength of over 970 pounds per square inch and most wet saws cannot cut this type of tile without excessive vibrations that cause chipping. Wet saws are only recommended when the cut area will be covered by more than ¼ inch of switch plate or molding. Using masking tape over the cutting line may minimize chipping.
  — *Information courtesy Arthur Mintie*

Figure 216. Troweling on adhesive.

Figure 217. Using spacers to leave the right space for grout.

Figure 218. Sponging off excess grout.

Figure 219. The best moment of all—viewing the completed tile installation.
Photos courtesy Sandhill Industries

Figure 220. Grout width affects a design. The wider the width, the more charmingly rustic and casual the look ... which is currently a very popular look. The more narrow the grout line, the finer the finished look. A current trend—a no-grout look—is seen with contemporary-looking large-format tiles.
Photo courtesy OriginalStyle

Chapter 7
Sources

Adagio Art Glass
www.adagioartglsss.com
Ann Sacks
www.annsacks.com
Art & Maison Miami
www.artandmaison.com
Artistic Tile
www.artistictile.com
Bedrock
www.bedrockindustries.com
Bisazza North America
www.bisazzausa.com
Boyce & Bean
www.boyceandbean.com
Country Floors
www.countryfloors.com
Crossville, Inc.
www.crossvilleinc.com
Diamond Tech Glass Tiles
www.DTGlassTiles.com
Dolce Glass Tile/Down To Earth Products, Inc.
www.dolceglasstile.com
Erin Adams Design Inc.
www.erinadamsdesign.com
GlasTile, Inc.
www.glastile.com
Hakatai Enterprises, Inc.
www.hakati.com
Interstyle
www.interstyle.ca
Jordan Goldstein, Gensler
www.bermanglasseditions.com
Kokomo Opalescent Glass Co., Inc.
www.kog.com
Laticrete
www.laticrete.com
Marin Designworks Glass Tile
www.marindesignworks.com
Mixed-Up-Mosaics
www.mixed-upmosaics.com
Old Hancock Glass Tile
Chris Baker-Salmon, Owner
Chris@OHGTile.com
Oceanside Glasstile
www.glasstile.com
Original Style
www.originalstyle.com
Angelo Orsoni SPA
www.orsoni.com
Orsoni Smalti Veneziana
North American Press Office
JoAnn Loctov
joannio@orsonio.com
Rosan Imports
Rudy Santos, Owner
RosanUSA@optonline.net
Sandhill Industries
www.sandhillind.com, e.m
Sicis
www.bettini.com
Trend Group
North American Press Office
JoAnn Loctov
joannio@orsonio.com
Trikeenan Tileworks, Inc.
www.trikeenan.com
Ultraglas Tile
www.ultraglas.com,
Vidrotil
www.vidrotil.com
Walker Zanger
www.lbtsdiego.com/Walker Zanger Store